San Diego Days

San Diego Days

Written & Illustrated
by
Bro Halff

Simpler Gifts Press, LLC
San Diego

Published in 2021 by Simpler Gifts Press, LLC
and Bro Halff Gallery Hawaii, LLC

For information, address the publishers:

Simpler Gifts Press, LLC
1050 Rosecrans Street, Suite D
San Diego, California 92106

Bro Halff Gallery Hawaii, LLC
1706 Keoniloa Place
Koloa, Hawaii 96756

Library of Congress Card Catalog Number
ISBN 978-1-885238-15-3

This book is dedicated to the people of San Diego,
kind friends and steadfast neighbors.

San Diego is a beautiful city at the southwestern tip of California. It has a colorful history that has been largely shaped since 1900 by the city's importance to the United States Navy, as well as by its proximity to Mexico. The computer science and biotech industries have played a major role in its growth in the last twenty years. Tourism remains an important economic force. It hosts several major universities and many fine smaller institutions of higher learning. Now the eighth-largest city in the United States, it has flourished in recent years, in large part because of its connections to technology, the military, and international trade.

Juan Rodriguez Cabrillo was the first European known to visit the San Diego area, in 1542. Cabrillo laid claim to San Diego Bay for Spain, but colonization of the region did not begin in earnest until 1769, when four parties of Spaniards arrived from the south. Governor-designate Gaspar de Portolá built a presidio, or fort, on a hill overlooking the San Diego River. Junipero Serra founded a mission, named San Diego de Alcalá, near the river. Mexico assumed control of San Diego when Mexico attained its independence from Spain in 1821. San Diego became part of the province known as Alta California. As a result of the Mexican-American War (1846-1848), the United States annexed Alta California, including San Diego, in 1848.

San Diego remained a fairly sleepy city until the U.S. Navy began to build major facilities there, starting in 1901. The aviation industry also boosted the growth of the city, as did the Panama-California Exposition (1915) and the California Pacific International Exposition (1935). Both were held in Balboa Park, which remains one of the most beautiful urban parks in the country. Tuna fishing and canning also fueled San Diego's growth. However, it was World War II, with its influx of military operations and personnel, that insured San Diego's status as one of California's largest cities.

San Diego almost certainly would have become a more prominent urban center earlier, had it not been for one geographical obstacle that it faces. To its east are rugged mountains and desert, which made construction of major rail lines to the east difficult and expensive. As a result, Los Angeles, about 120 miles to the north, became the railway terminus that primarily connected areas east of California to the Pacific Ocean and its busy West Coast ports.

I moved to San Diego from the Los Angeles area in 1986, after growing up in Texas and living for years in the East and Midwest. I had visited San Diego many times before moving there, and I was always intrigued by its "small-town" atmosphere, its natural and manmade beauty, and its relaxed pace of life. I lived in San Diego until 2006, when I moved to Hawaii. I came to love San Diego, although by the time I left, its growth had somewhat overshadowed the relaxed lifestyle that initially had appealed to me.

When I first moved to San Diego, a friend advised me that San Diego was "120 miles south of L.A. and 100 years earlier," in terms of its lifestyle. I found this generalization to be generally true. I had envisioned San Diego as a smaller version of Los Angeles, but the two cities are, or at least were, completely dissimilar.

San Diego is an unconventional and surprising city. Its climate, at least within five miles of the coast, was once described to me as having only one season – early spring. This characterization is accurate. It is consistently cool and breezy, with pervasive fog, especially near the coast, for at least a third, and sometimes half, of the year. Winters generally bring sunnier days, punctuated by rainstorms that arrive from the north from time to time.

I found people in San Diego to be sometimes very private, although outwardly friendly. A friend once told me, shortly after I had moved there, that everyone who moved to San Diego had done so in pursuit of a personal dream, and that because these dreams were all so distinct, it was sometimes hard to discern a spirit of community, or a shared sense of identity. While there are many exceptions, I found this generally to be the case.

San Diego is a city that does not readily reveal its greatest charms, despite its appearance of cordiality and beauty. Nevertheless, its elusive qualities are there, and have deeply influenced my life. There is a graceful beauty in Balboa Park, in the sometimes-boisterous beach communities, in the rugged "back country" east of

San Diego, and in the many haunts that San Diego's harbor, its Mission Bay, and its distinctive communities offer to the patient observer.

This book, along with its companion volume, *San Diego Visions,* is my attempt to reveal to the viewer and reader, in paintings and poetry, some of the insights – about places and people – that San Diego has bestowed on me. It is as much a book about a time as about a place, because the San Diego of the late twentieth and early twenty-first centuries was more of a shy friend than the bold companion that the city has increasingly become. Both types of acquaintances have their merits and their rewards. However, I feel fortunate to have known a San Diego that was more isolated, yet also more intimate and tied to its past, than is the current metropolis. I hope that the reader will enjoy my rambles through quiet neighborhoods, peaceful parks, and rugged back country, as well as to scenic overlooks and historic landmarks.

As important as these scenes are to me, the people whom I met and came to cherish along the way are even more meaningful to me. These friends and strangers taught me to observe and enjoy moments of deep emotion and unexpected insight, moments that life offers to all of us, when we are willing to recognize them. I have sought to capture some of these occasions in words, as I have striven to portray in images the sights that were precious, and still remain meaningful, to me. San Diego, in my imagination and in my memory of my life there, is as vivid and uplifting as it was when I loved living there.

A California Overlook

An old tower,
with its stern
weathervane
and water-stained
walls,
rises
above a tile-festooned
dome,
which has painted
its belly
into a bubble
adorned with jellybeans.

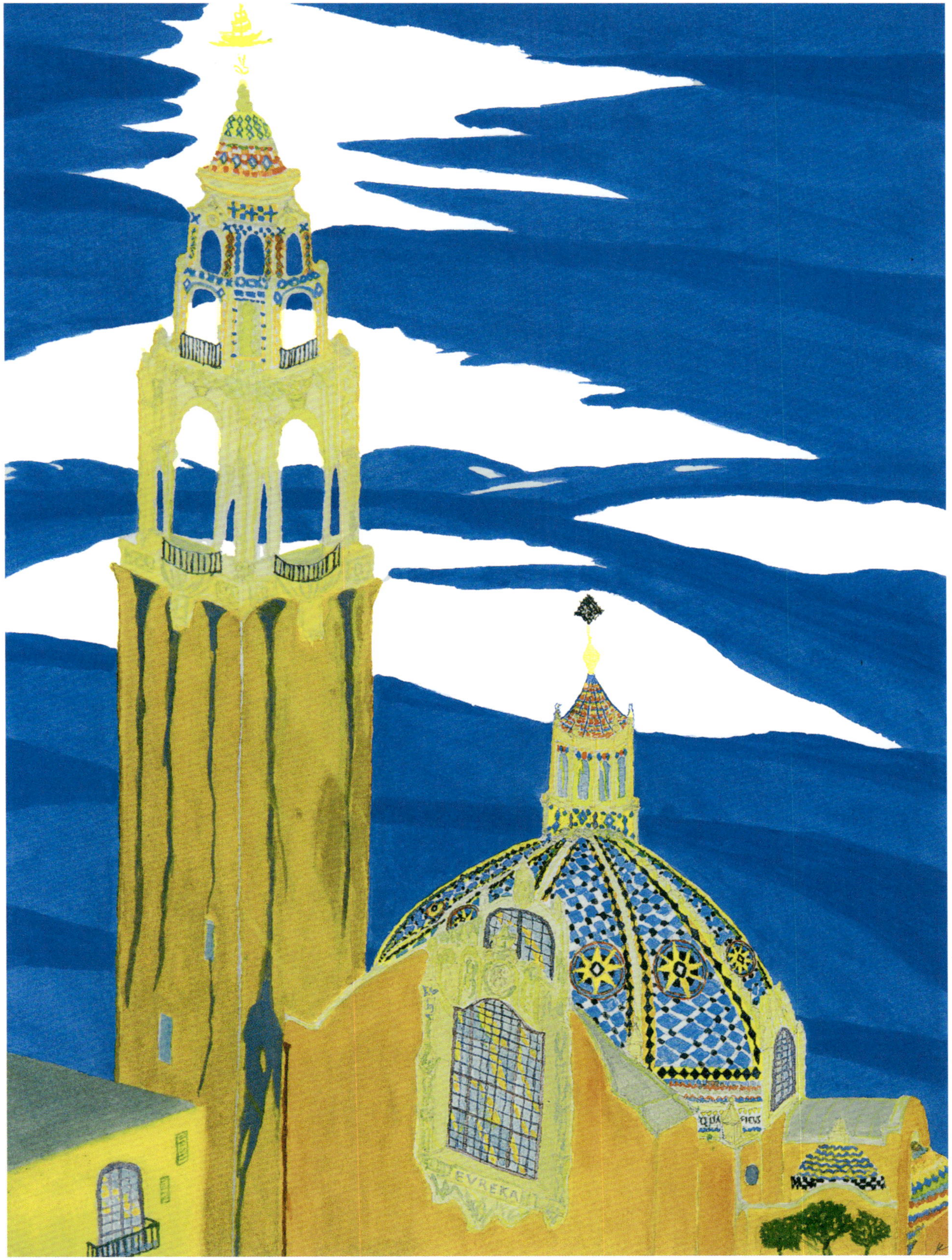
EVREKA

Growing Up Happy

The undersides
of the maple
sapling's
leaves
flutter
in silver
beauty,
under a full moon's
gaze;
trembling
to the touches
of breezes,
they whisper
and smile
at the sky,
which, overburdened
with stars,
bends
low,
to watch
a leaf
kick up
its heels,
and dance its way
out of the reach
of sharp-tongued
branches.

A Good Ear

A blind woman
with an accordion
sits
in a lounge chair
on the sidewalk,
with an open coffee can
before her;
and, even above the belly laughs
of her instrument,
she can hear
the difference
between giggling coins
and bills
that whisper
their applause.

Fragrant Devotion

On Sunday
morning,
I pause
on my walk,
to smell
the roses
of neighbors
who are praying
in church –
perhaps
they will forgive me
my weekend
dalliance,
with light-hearted believers
in red-petaled
redemption,
and yellow-blossomed
rebirth.

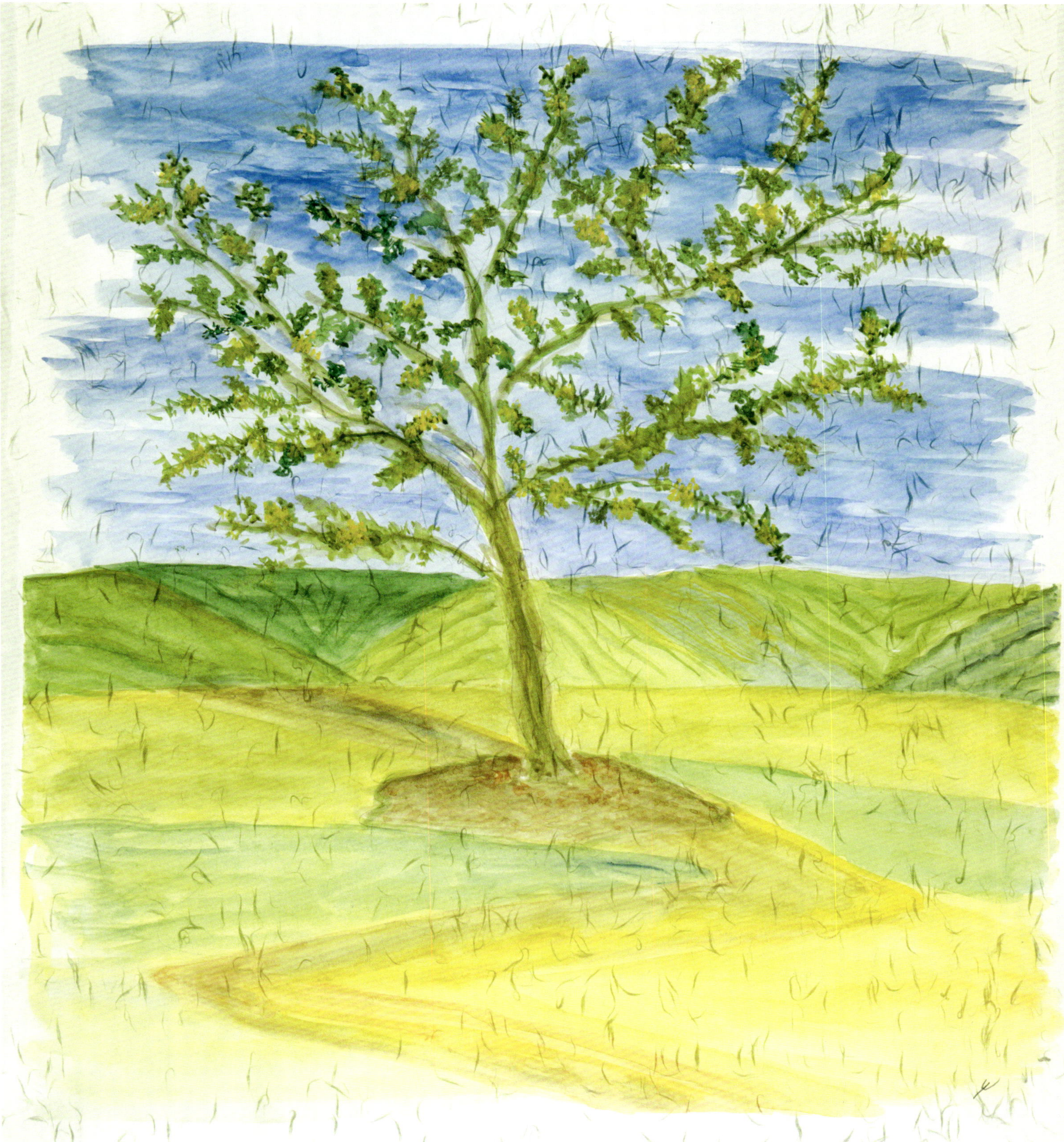

Bright-Eyed Believers

Pelicans,
fishing
in a sunlight-dappled
ocean,
dive
and soar,
then dive again,
and, getting their bearings,
float
on the waves,
waiting
for a flicker of silver
to call them
to dinner,
on an afternoon
when clouds
cast their shadow nets,
and catch
agile
schools
of sunfish.

Sailing Home

A clear day
under a bright-eyed sun
rests
in the lap
of the ocean:
waves make their way
to a green-skirted
shore,
while the horizon
dawdles,
before swimming away,
as clouds
cast down
their shadows,
planting islands
across the Pacific,
bequeathing stepping stones
to sun-weary
mariners.

A Monday Catch

Up and down
the fishing pier,
the rods
and reels
send their lines
streaking,
while behind them
patient
anglers
wait,
for a tug
from the depths
of heaven.

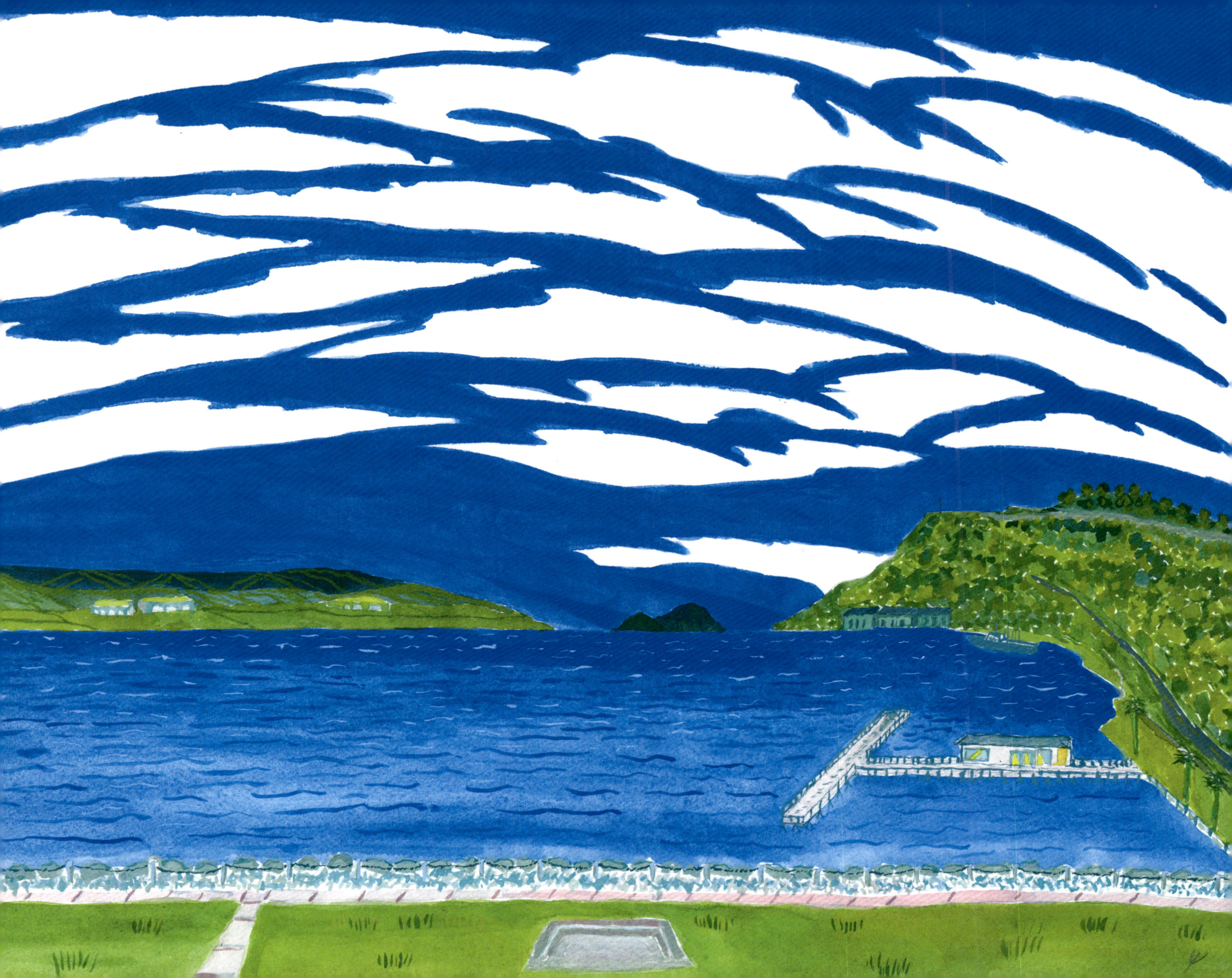

Heading Home

The ocean,
the port,
the town
climbing hills,
and over all,
a blue sky,
promising
marriages –
the land
listens
to waves whisper,
and furls
the white sails
of its clouds,
as a warm day
awakens,
and mountains
leave deserts
behind them,
to gaze
out to sea
at an island
of westering
light.

Reflected Glory

The city
basks
in late light,
which gilds
skyscrapers
and old buildings,
wharves
and steamships,
while above them,
a shy moon
emerges,
touching
the harbor
with its silver
wand,
leaving
the skyline
to wrap itself
in shadows,
while facing
the water
with a parting
smile
of golden
remembrance.

Twilight Festivities

The city
in late sunlight,
casting its gaze
across the harbor,
glistens,
as the sky
lights birthday candles,
to celebrate
another day,
while the tide
pulls up stakes
and elopes
with the horizon-crossing
ocean.

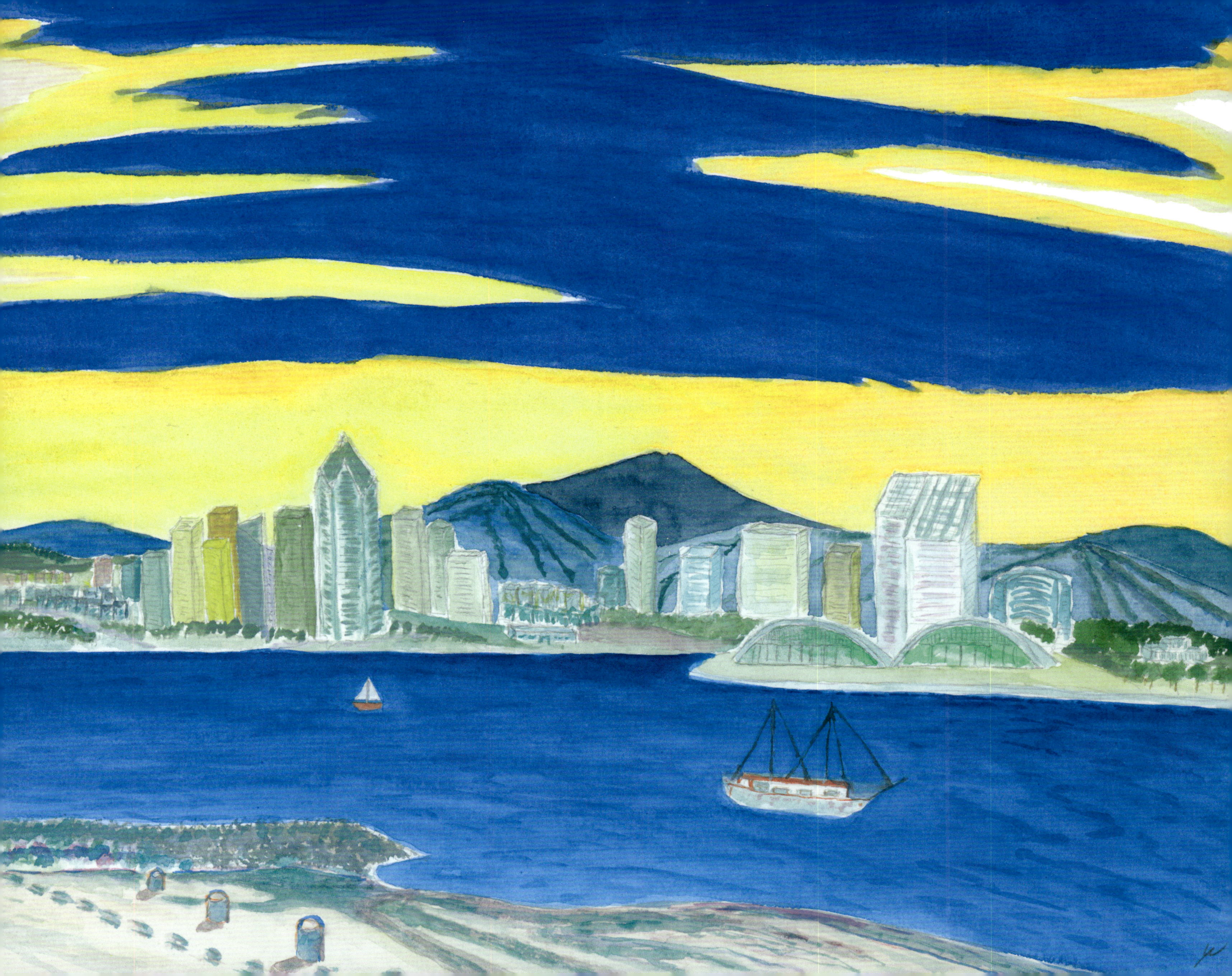

Old California

A valley
on the west side
of the mountains
basks
in winter sunlight –
opening its palm
to the wise
and the weary,
it outstretches
a golden coin
that is anyone's
for the seeking.

A Flight of Fancy

A solitary
robin,
hopping
across the grass,
catches sight
of a bare limb
that invites him
to take flight,
to let his wings
be its dark leaves,
his belly
its autumn
plumage.

Homecomings

Blue skies
at the horizon
offer
their promise
of hope –
with no pretension,
they stretch out
to doze,
while clouds
bed down
with one another,
and the land
follows roads
to little towns
that open
their laps,
to a tentmaker
who got stuck
with too much
blue canvas.

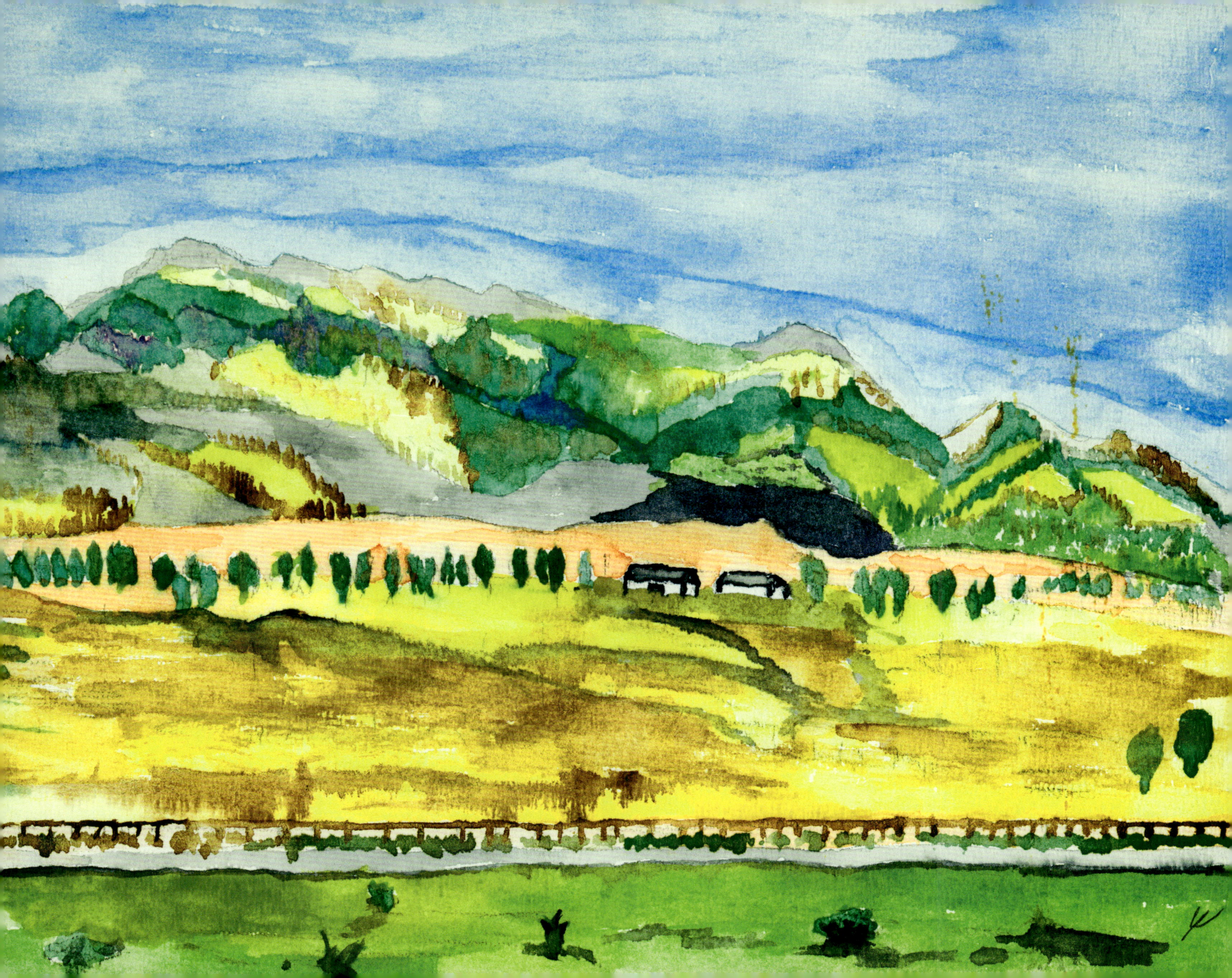

A Calm Voyage

The ocean,
dozing
on a sunny day,
sets out
for distant shores,
and if it does not reach
a green-skirted island,
still it will daydream,
under a sky
where stars
float
on pillows.

A May Romance

Green land
and winding rivers
embrace one another,
keeping watch
for each other,
as the purple cloak
of evening
covers them both,
until the first stars
come courting
the fields,
and the moon
offers its smile
to a stream
that welcomes its suitor
with a flattering
mirror.

Setting Out

Late sunlight
far out to sea
pools
beyond
banks of fog –
there, in the distance,
it beckons
the onlooker,
promising
a land
where dawn
keeps it promises.

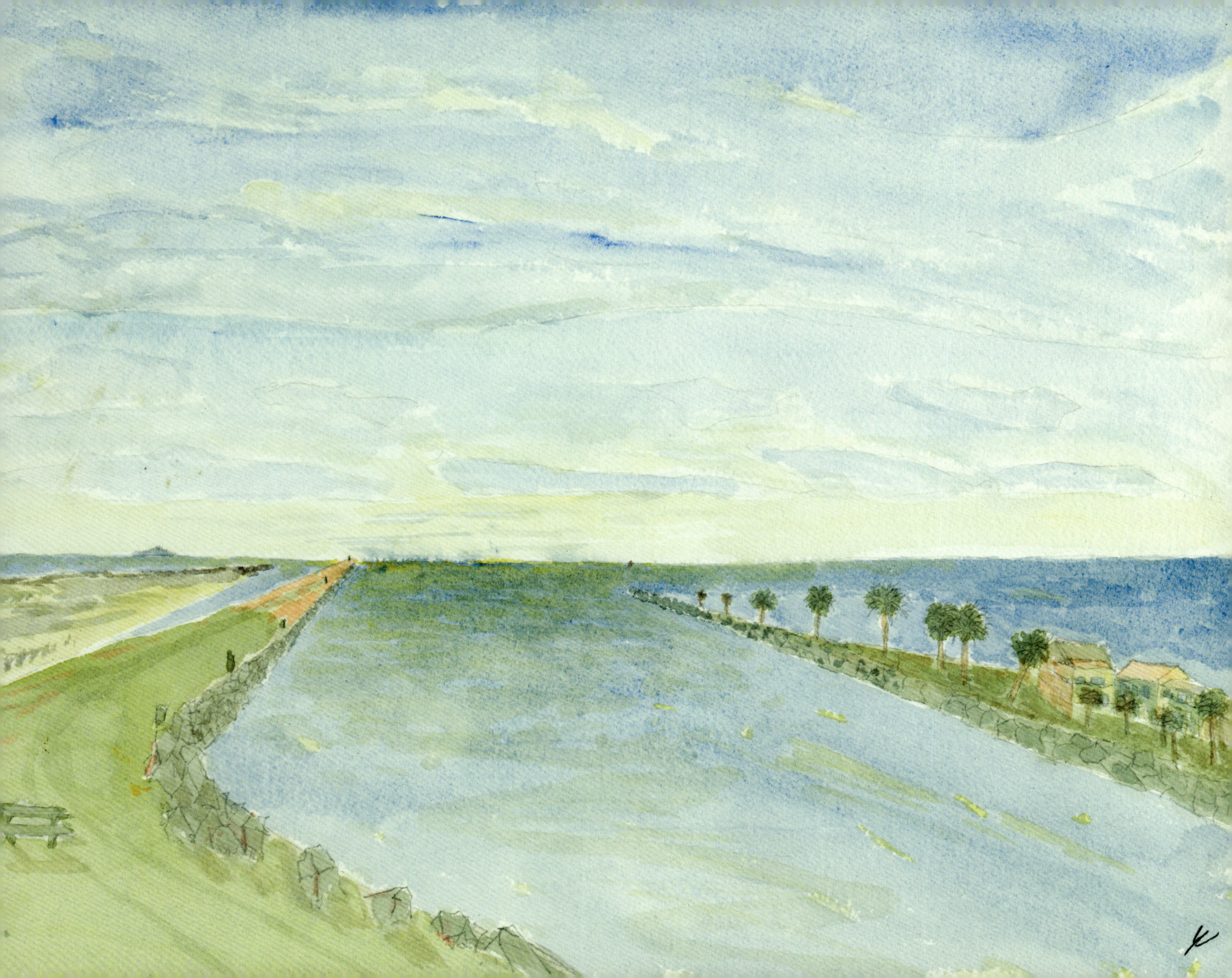

Delicate Kisses

Rain
peppers
a red tile roof,
telegraphing
its message
of spring
innuendos,
of suggestions
of downpours
of blossoms,
while the roof,
enjoying
the rush
of water
across its face,
sputters,
as a torrent
plummets
to the ground,
where it gurgles
at the thought
of a waterfall
of undelivered
love letters.

The Whole Truth

Two red roses,
blossoming
together
and apart,
never forget
to perfume
the same
sidewalk,
to answer
the love letters
that breezes
and bees
exchange
for them.

Without Translation

Houses
from other lands
cluster
in a circle –
beneath orange-tiled
roofs,
they open
their blue doors
and yellow shutters,
to welcome
gusts
of palm trees'
laughter.

International Houses, Balboa Park

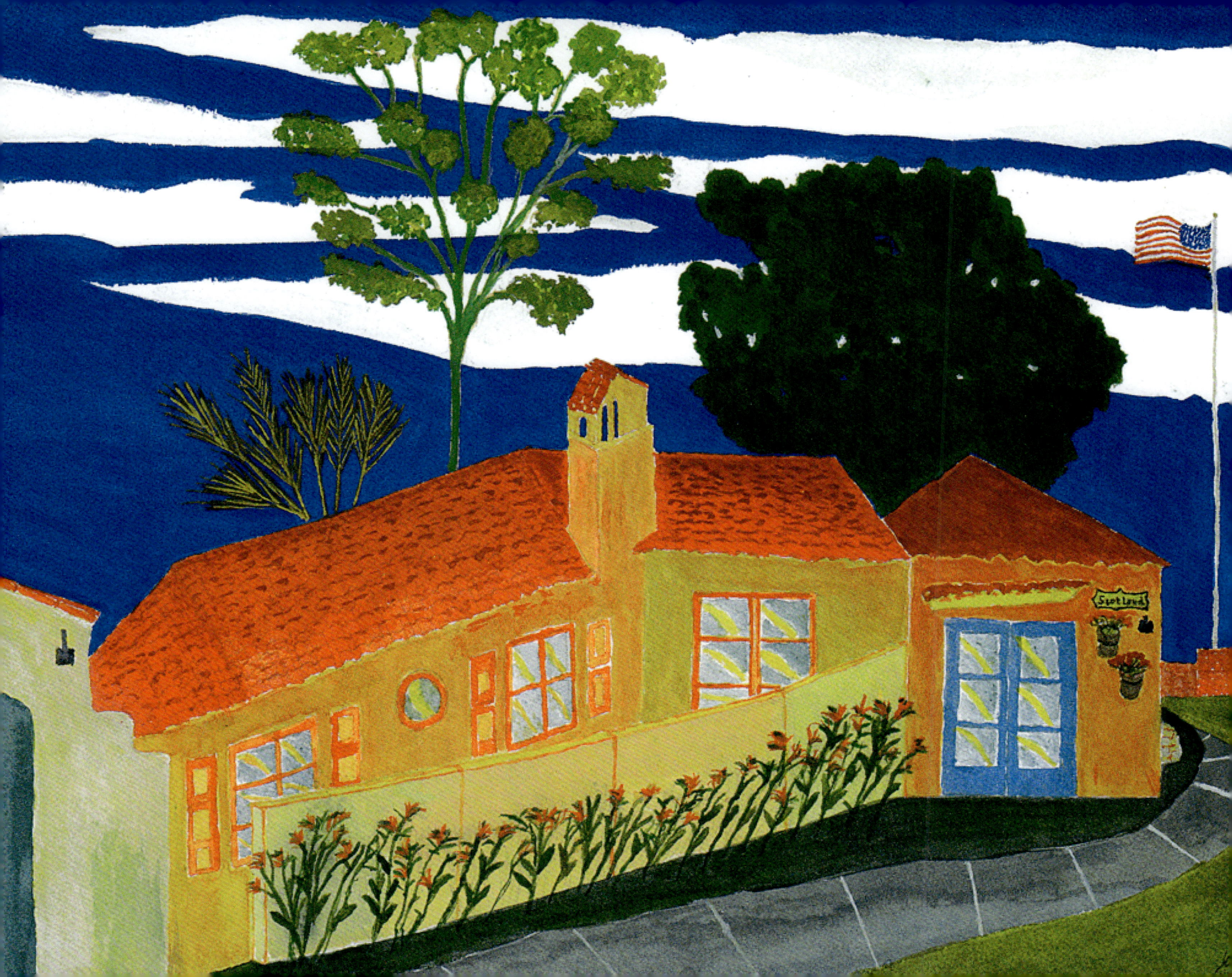

A Morning Romance

The surf
strokes the beach
with calm
fingertips,
whispering
the same
tender song:
over and over
it repeats
the refrain –
take pity,
take heart,
awaken
in my arms.

The sand
is a believer
in lovers
who arrive
bearing dreams.

More than Fruit

An old Cherokee woman
with braided gray hair
and a soft voice
smiles
as she offers you
an orange –
what a gift
she extends
with her words –
"An orange,"
she says,
and it glows.

A Calm Shore

The sky
has raised
its blue and white
flag,
bright-striped
and adventurous,
above the open-armed
ocean –
before the sky and the sea,
the brown land
settles down
for a nap,
content
to stay home,
and let breezes
whisper
of runaway
islands.

Pump Station 35, San Diego

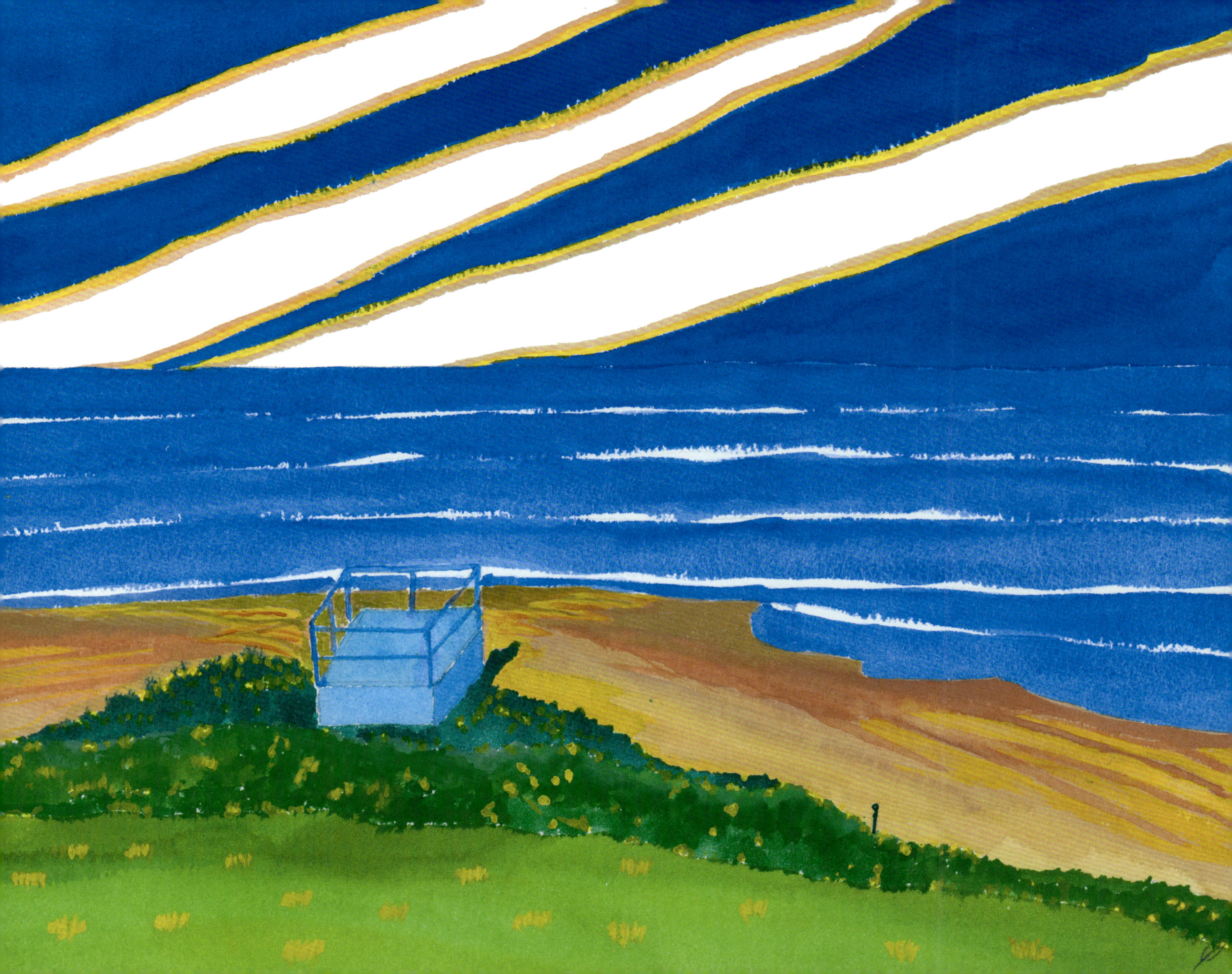

Down Coverlets

Two ducks,
resting
in the grass,
tuck
themselves in,
one
in a pool of shade,
the other
in an ocean
of light.

Sweet Somethings

What
would life be
without a stick
of chewing gum,
a sweet wad
of elastic laughter,
massaging
the tough
back teeth?

What
would hold
the world together,
when it all
has turned
to doubt,
if there were
no stick
of sugary
glue,
patching up
a solemn gaze,
and turning it
into a smile?

Under the Sun

A yellow building
beside a palm tree
admires itself
in a reflecting pond –
gazing down,
it watches
its smile
shimmer,
while above the two
proud companions,
a modest sky
builds its own blue heaven
out of rough-hewn
beams of light.

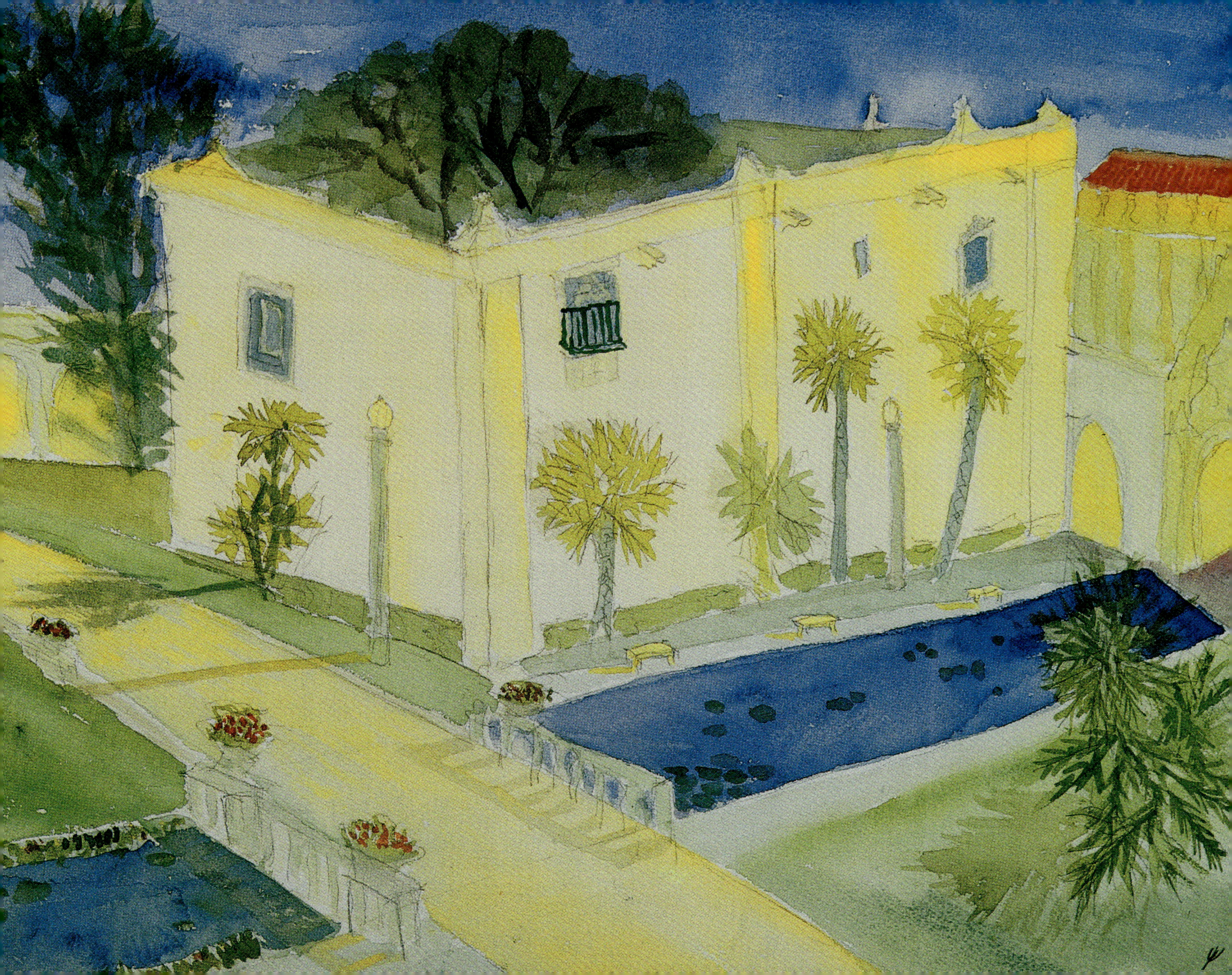

Making Room for Laughter

The black-leafed
plum tree,
where last summer
the ardent bees
flourished,
has split
and grown
sickly,
with withered
branches
and shriveled
leaves,
and though no golden bees
now crown it
with their haloes,
the July sunlight
seeks it out,
to rest
in its open arms,
its empty honeycomb
with a gaping smile
and a sweet tooth.

Early Spring

The breeze
rises
late in the afternoon,
serenading
a copse of trees,
where robins
carol,
and the leaves
sigh
their accompaniment.

Easy Steps

Before dawn,
the eastern sky
hikes up its skirts
and dances,
scattering light
in every direction,
as the stars,
growing faint,
swing each other
out of sight,
until the sun
waltzes
over a hill,
and the land
partners
every timid tree
with a graceful
shadow.

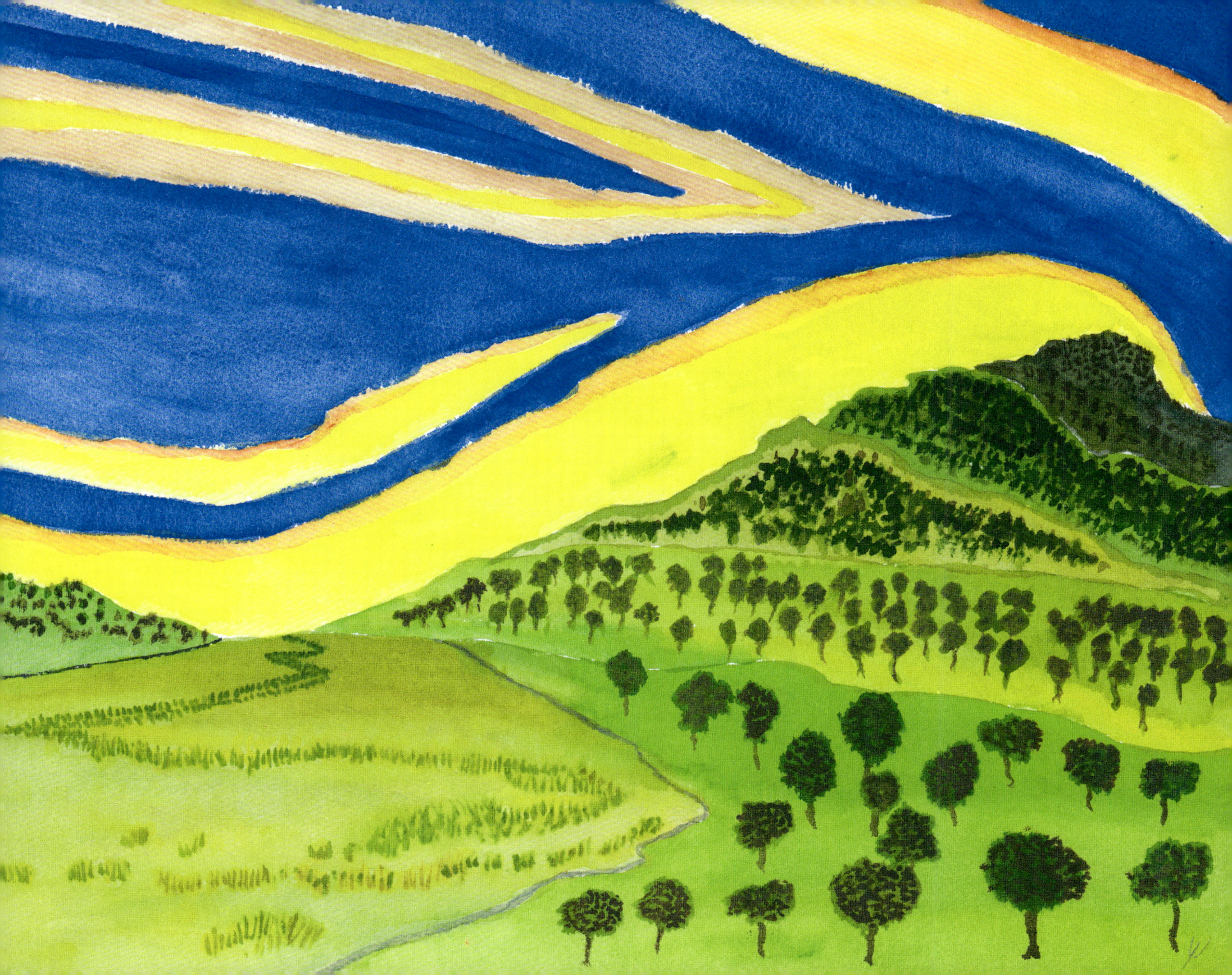

Nimbus

The Pacific Ocean
under a cloud-speckled
sky
beams
at an arc
of light
so high
that it marries
waves
to the ocean's
halo.

The Iliad

Homer,
intent
on telling the story
of gods
and honor,
never confuses
the demands
of the two,
for one
shakes heaven and earth
to triumph,
while the other
weeps
at the thought
of disgrace.

Homer
gives each
their say,
which is why
kind fate
struck him
blind.

Coastal Companions

Point Loma
outstretches
its hand
to the ocean,
a traveler
who has journeyed
all day,
and who answers
the greeting
with an honest
handshake,
for a friend
who has kept
a sunrise promise,
to meet
every evening
at dusk.

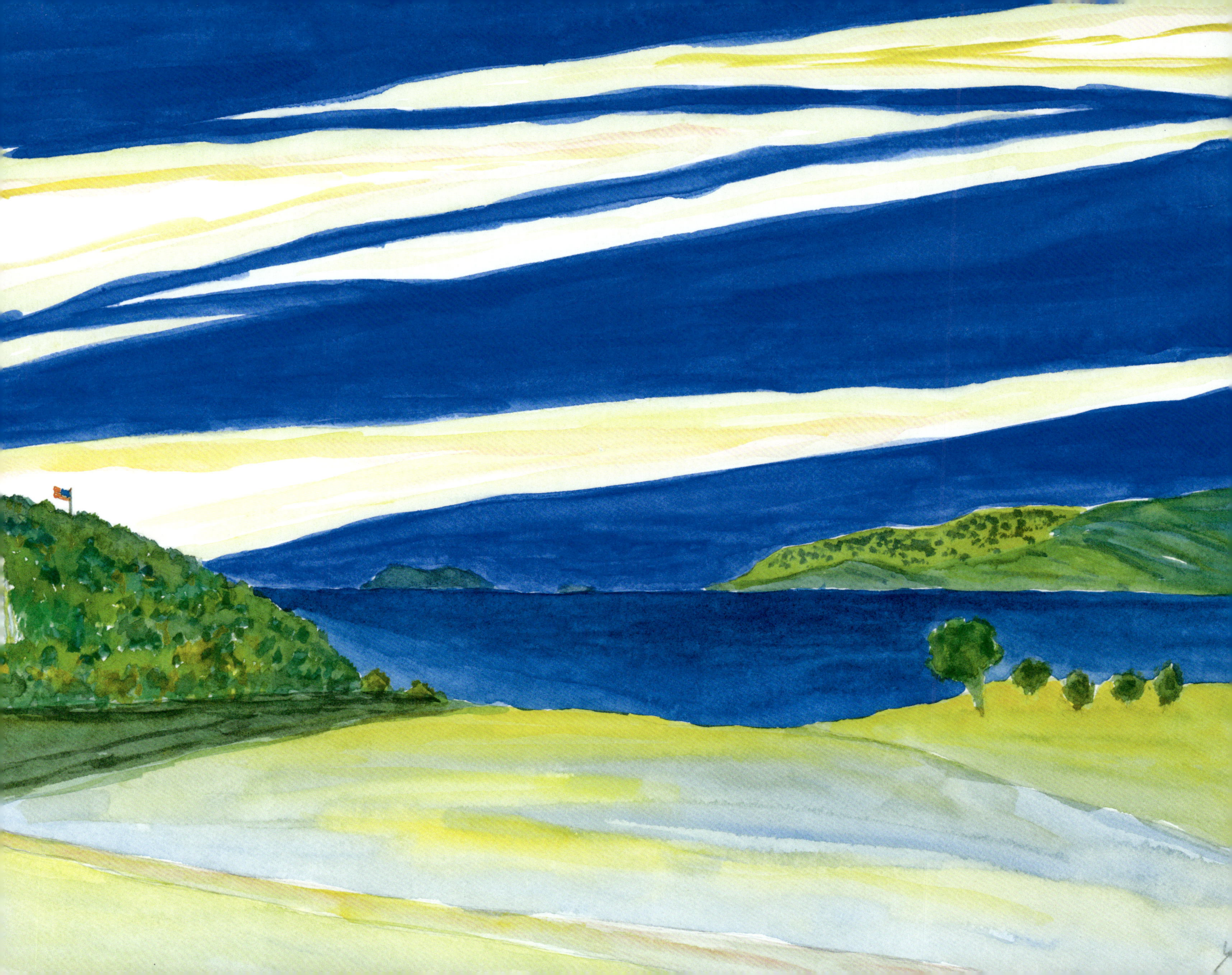

Upstairs

Home,
a beautiful
corner
of the world,
beckons
when you least
expect it,
singing to you
all night
in the trees
and the waves,
as you doze off
and awaken,
finding your bed
warm
to the touch,
and the sky
outside your window
cluttered
with stars.

Coming True

Light
on the ocean,
roaming
beyond the farthest
shadows
of clouds,
flashes
in the palms
of waves,
which are quick
to give away
their fortune,
to a horizon
that dreams
of sailing
into paradise.

Setting Out

A salmon house
gazes out,
past the points
and the headlands,
at an ocean
so calm
that it invites
the land
to swim
in its indigo
bathtub.

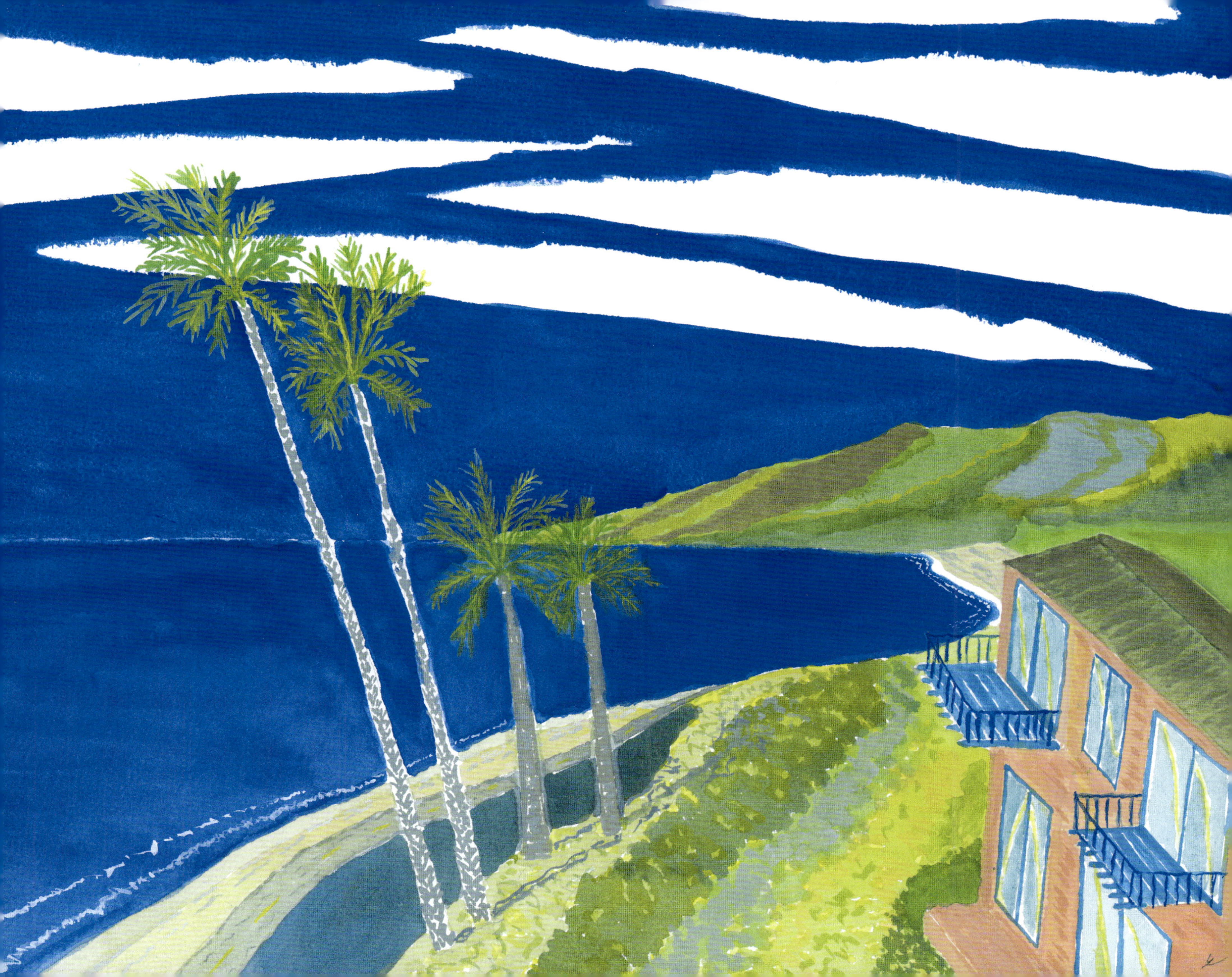

Binding Light

Dawn
creeps
across the horizon,
hiding its light
until the last
possible moment –
then, in a flash,
the lantern
is lit,
as the day
springs
to life,
and the land
pitches
its green tents,
while the clouds
roll out
their cotton candy
stands.

A Humble Miracle

On Christmas Eve,
three dogs
in the garage,
anxious to play,
have chewed up
an old broom,
scattering straw
everywhere,
transforming the garage
into a manger,
flooded with sunlight
on Christmas
at dawn,
where three joyful spaniels
cock their heads,
panting with excitement
over the birth
of a new day.

A Bright Moment

The beach
in sunlight,
the sand
turning coral,
a white halo
of fog
at the horizon,
the waves
mulling over
their azure
thoughts,
all
have their say,
their chance
to tell their stories,
on a shore
where the ocean
dances with driftwood.

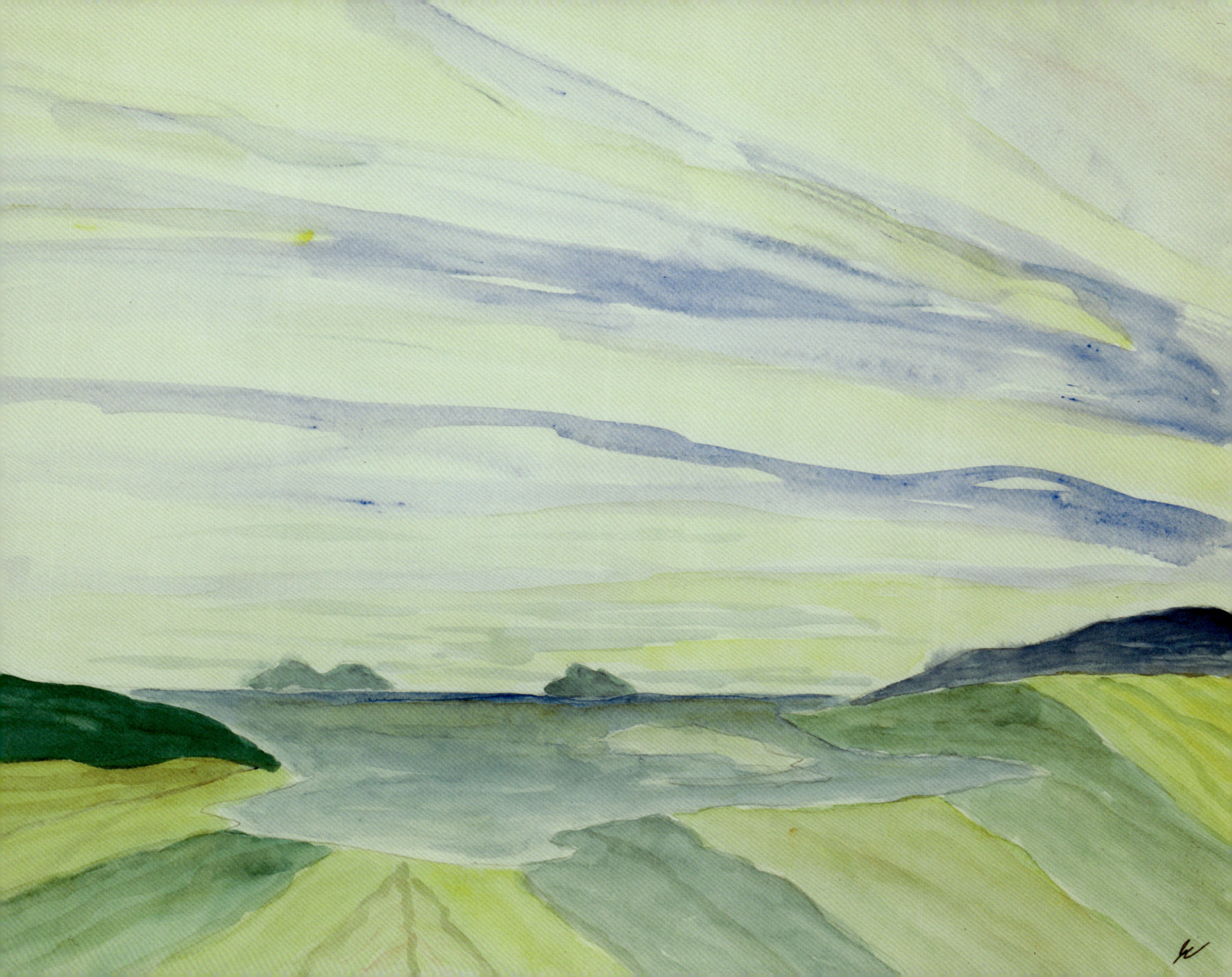

Inside and Out

A yellow house
on a yellow block
dozes
under a brilliant
sun –
beyond
the façade's
faded smile,
a garden
rages
in the shade
of a red
hydrangea.

Kind Music

Night
after night,
the dishwasher
consoles me
with its roar
and its clatter –
gargling
and spitting
and clearing
its throat,
it speaks up
on bad nights,
when sleep
comes too late –
its gravel-throated
voice,
astir
in the kitchen,
makes me welcome
its long pauses,
as it listens
for the humming
of the down-to-earth
refrigerator.

An Antique Gentleman

An old house
with yellow trim
stands up straight,
with its broad shoulders
squared
against the sky,
and, glancing
at its tumbledown street,
from eyes
that do not blink,
offers
to a cluster
of violets
a gray umbrella
of shade.

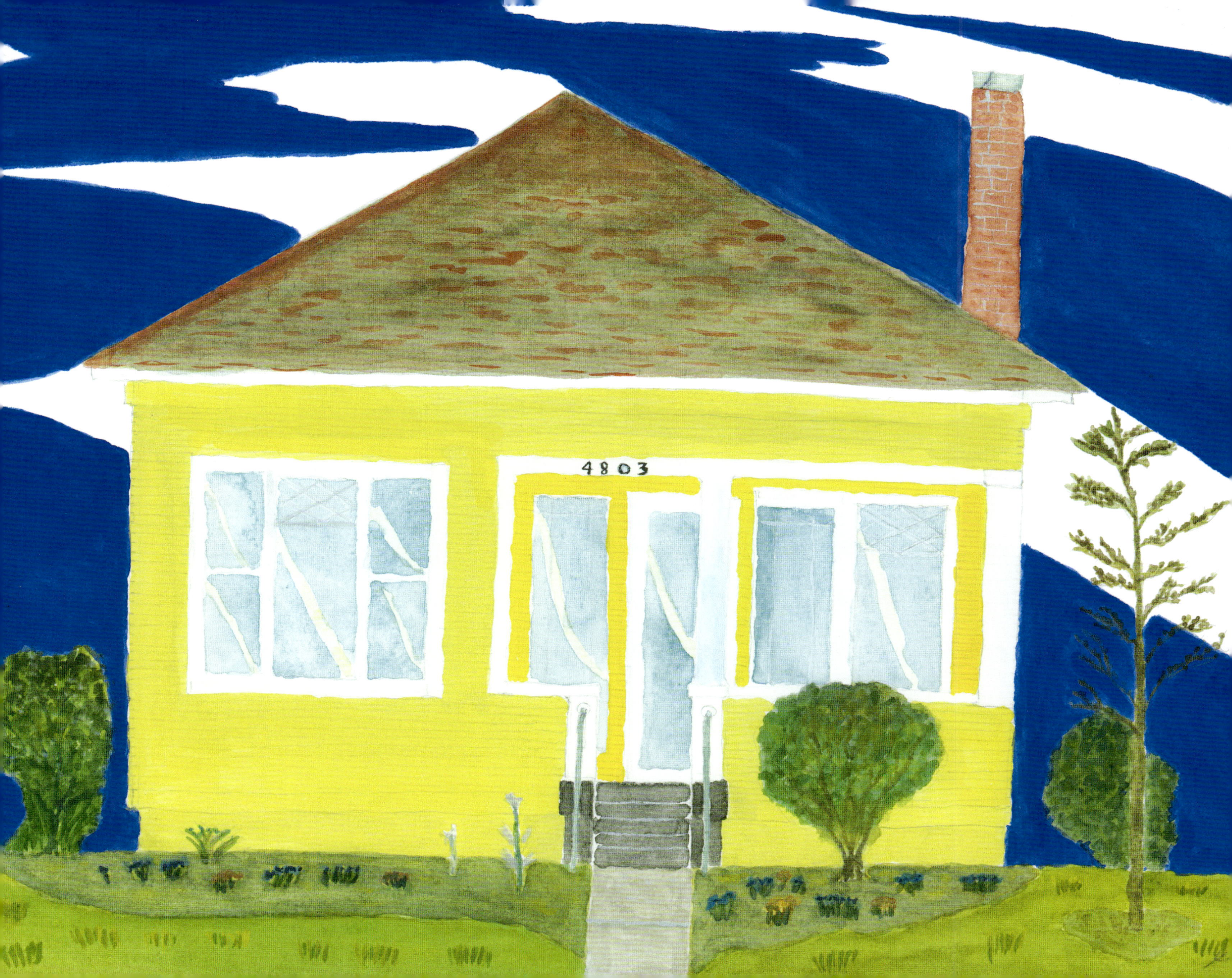
4803

On Vacation

Idle clouds,
puffed up
or down-to-earth,
laze
in a blue sky,
as the wind
pampers them,
and they,
leaning back,
enjoy
their far-flung
journeys,
their trips
to distant shores,
where mountains
tickle
their bellies.

Heading Home

A middle-aged man
wearing a baseball cap
maneuvers
among his young children,
his wife,
his sister-in-law
and five
takeout meals –
sporting
a taut smile,
he sits down
with the family
that he has herded
together
in the park –
sighing,
he smiles,
while the kids
squabble,
and his wife
talks
on her cell phone,
and his sister-in-law
reads
a tear-shedding novel.

With his puzzle of wrinkles
and his coffee-stained
T-shirt,
he looks around
at his unruly
empire,
wondering whether
the sports-hoarding TV
and beer-slinging
refrigerator
still wait for their midnight
date with him.

Stumbling Home

Mountains
and more mountains,
climbing
higher
and higher,
adorn themselves
with sunlight,
and with haloes
of clouds,
until they run out
of daredevil
stunts,
and tumble
without ceremony
into the lap
of the ocean,
which welcomes them
with the whispered praise
of modest
blue skies.

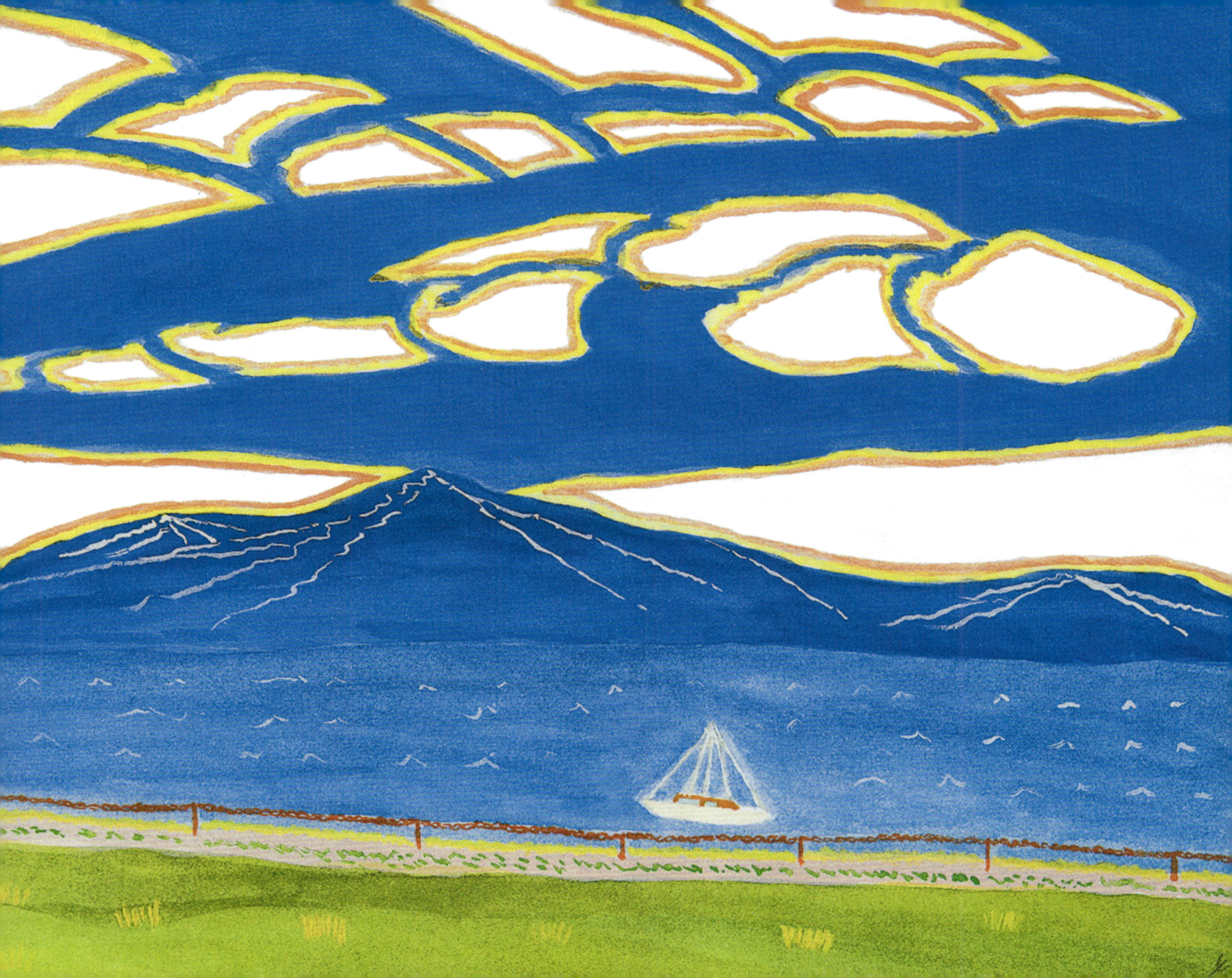

Moving On

And time,
so quick
to pass judgment
on a moment,
changes
in an instant
one life
and another,
until there is no way
to speak of the past,
as the days
find a new pace,
and the land
holds its own,
and the thrill
of the future
is its hasty
retreat.

Glee

Brushing out
two old dogs' coats
on a rainy
Saturday evening,
you give them
a few moments
of pleasure,
and yourself
an eternity
of dancing
with shaggy
moonlight.

Little Ado About Something

An old clock
oversees
a courtyard,
where a theater
welcomes
the Bard's
echoes,
while the clock,
not concerned
with time,
rests
in a bed
of blue
petunias.

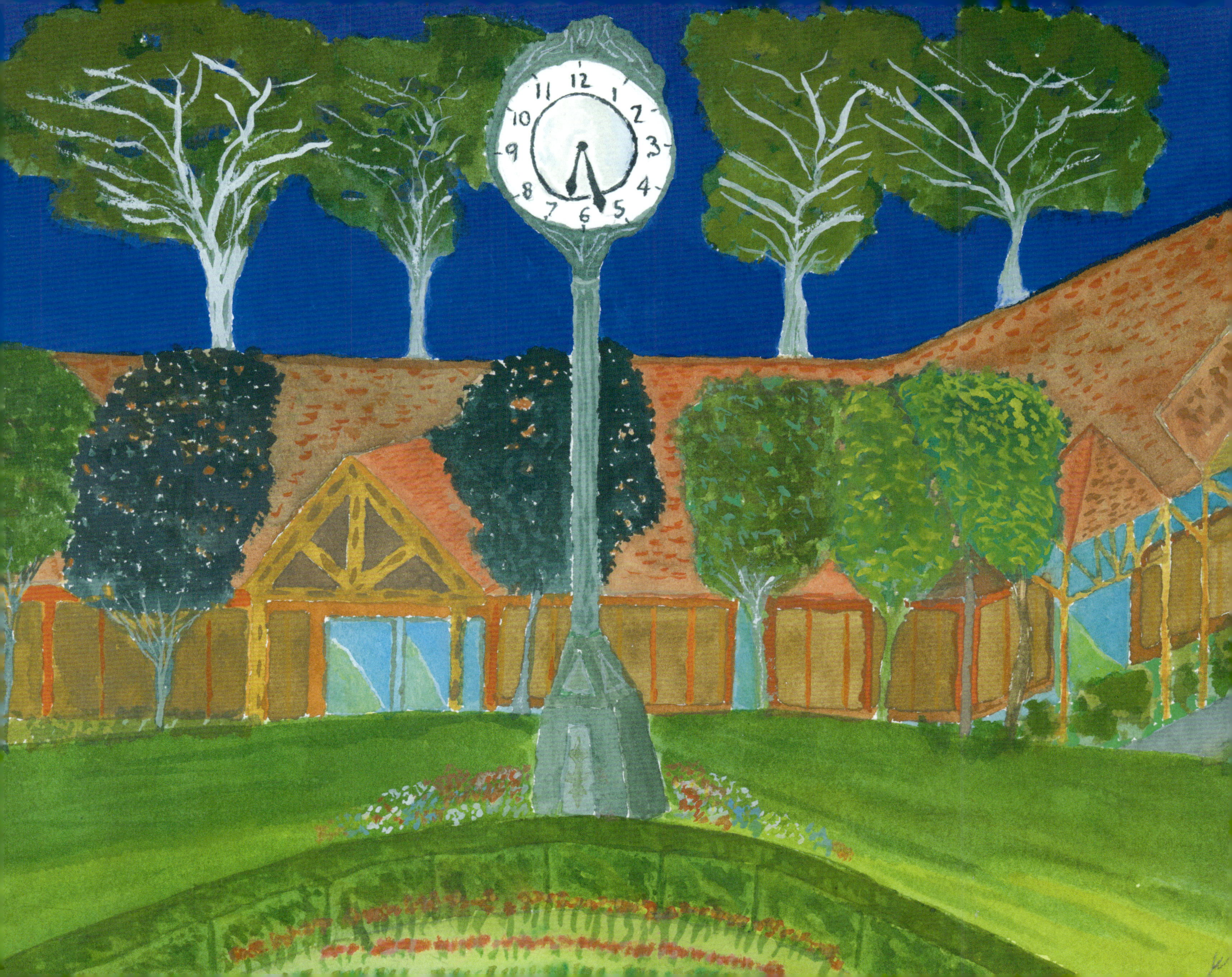

Inheriting a Fortune

The canyon
in morning sunlight,
gentle-hearted
among the shadows
of live oaks,
opens its arms
to a forest
of paths,
each speckled
with golden coins,
which spendthrift
branches
squander
day after day.

New Acquaintances

"Happy New Year,
and all that!"
snaps an old woman
to her neighbor,
as she starts
her morning walk,
along her unflinching
route.

Tired
of all the holiday hoopla,
she trudges
down the sunlit street,
scowling
beneath her visored
cap,
at a block
where a little boy
scampers
up the sidewalk,
and a whole new set
of robins
sing,
on telephone wires
above which the sky
turns cartwheels.

May

At last
the jacaranda trees
have blossomed,
opening
their lavender
parasols,
to greet
a sky
grown gray
from waiting,
for a downpour
of starry-eyed
petals.

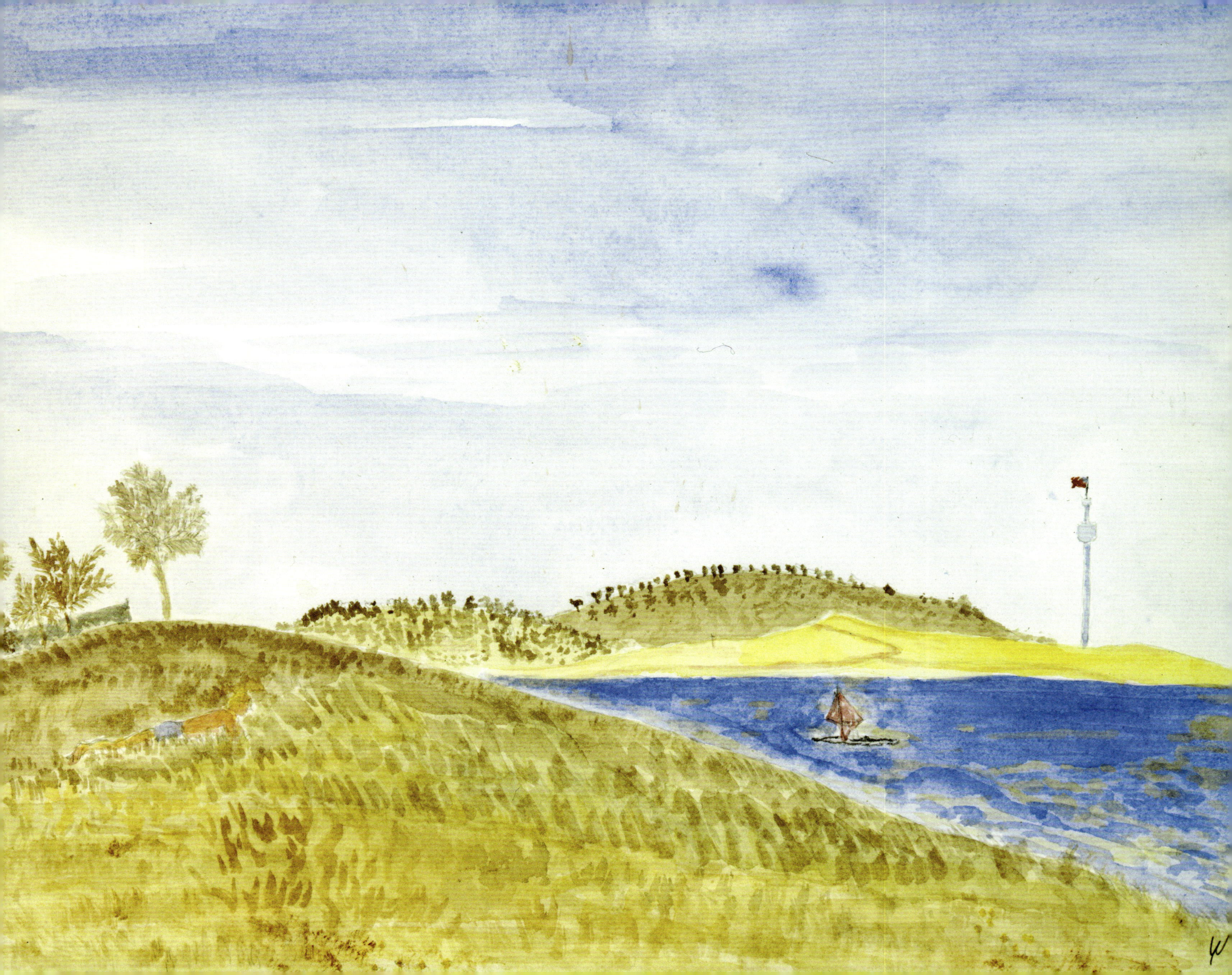

Gratis

A ragtag man
sits
on a park bench,
nursing
his cigarette,
as he coaxes
sunlight
out
from behind the clouds –
leaning back
on a November day
after Thanksgiving,
he stubs out
his smoke,
then takes
a deep breath
of air
that is traveling light,
with high-flying
Christmas gifts.

Obscure Gifts

A clam digger
in late afternoon,
a solitary
man,
sinks his shovel
into the sand,
then smiles
at a purple cloud,
behind which the sun
is catnapping.

Beginnings

Young trees,
leafing out
in early spring,
unfurl
their green pennants,
their messengers
of joy,
and, letting their limbs
bob,
nod
to the sunlight,
to the undaunted
blue sky,
with its high-flying
white kites
of clouds.

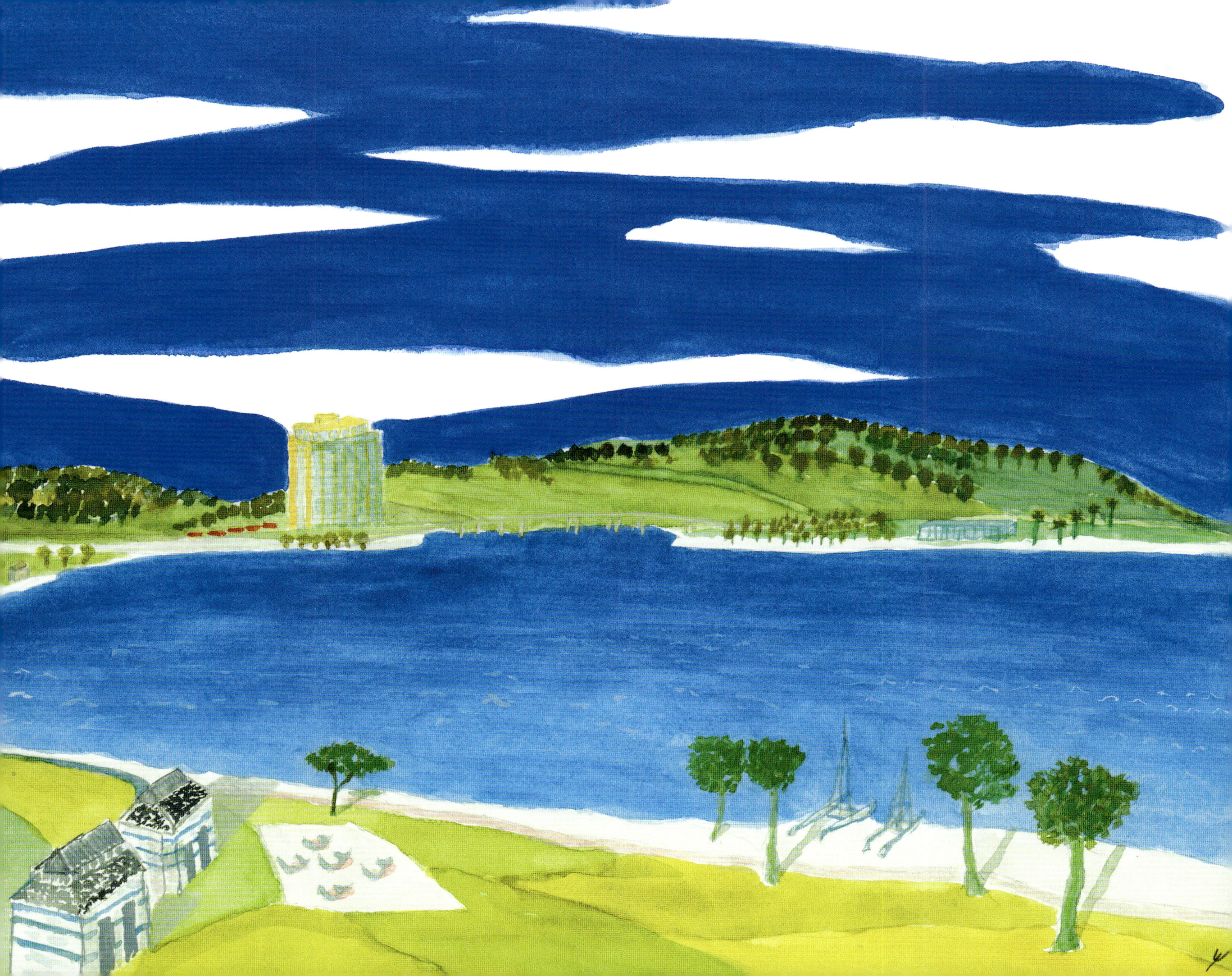

Finding Their Way

A sailboat,
riding
home
at dusk,
unfurls its sail
to the last of the light –
a white flag
before the purple horizon
signals
the boat's
surrender,
to breezes
that will sleep
in the arms
of mountains.

Setting Himself Free

An old man
walks his Golden Retriever
on a sunny
Sunday morning,
letting the dog
meander
from one tuft of grass
to another,
as the man's eyes
stray
beyond the jagged coastline,
to a pair of sailboats
that venture
out of reach
of any owner,
except the gadabout
wind.

Getting Away

A blue bridge
and a yellow island
abide,
while behind them,
an indigo mountain
shrugs its shoulders,
and in its lap,
a turquoise bay
wallows:
there a red and white sailboat
tugs
at its anchor,
for the sake
of all four
of its dressed-to-go
neighbors.

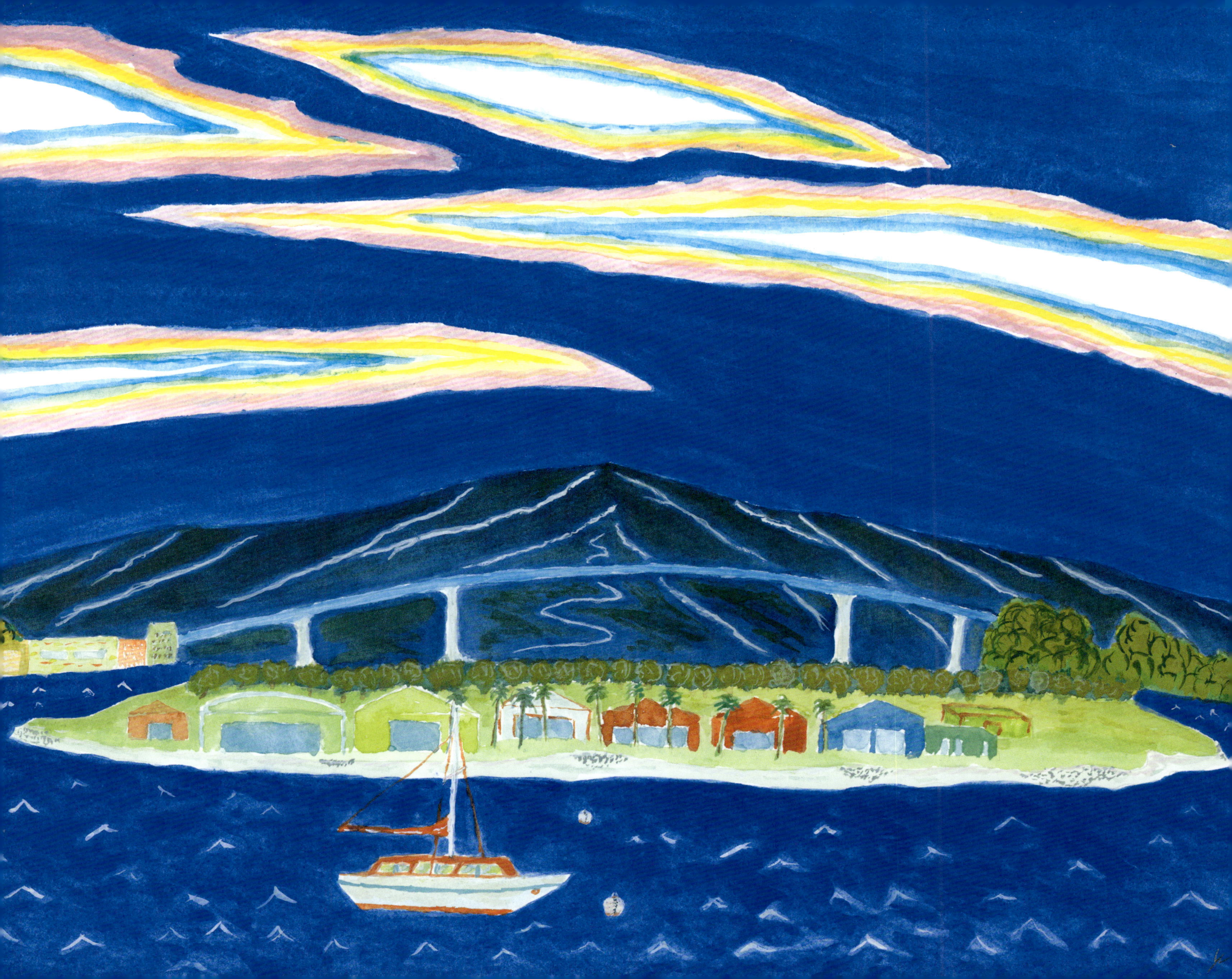

Realist

A middle-aged woman
with calm
blonde hair
sits
on a park bench,
while a white pigeon
sits at her feet,
cooing
and watching –
she gazes out
at the white-winged ocean,
home to flamboyant sailboats,
while she prefers
the company
of a down-to-earth
green bench,
and a bird
that flutters to life,
if she so much
as opens her purse.

Finding Her Way

A young woman
stands
on a sunlit beach,
swinging
her baby
in a circle,
making the needle
of her makeshift
compass
dance
about the North Pole
of her sky-high
laughter.

The Crystal Pier

The blue pier
from another era
points its finger
at the horizon,
blaming it
for the disappearance
of cotton-candy
clouds,
and sea-bathers
buoyed up
by bloomers.

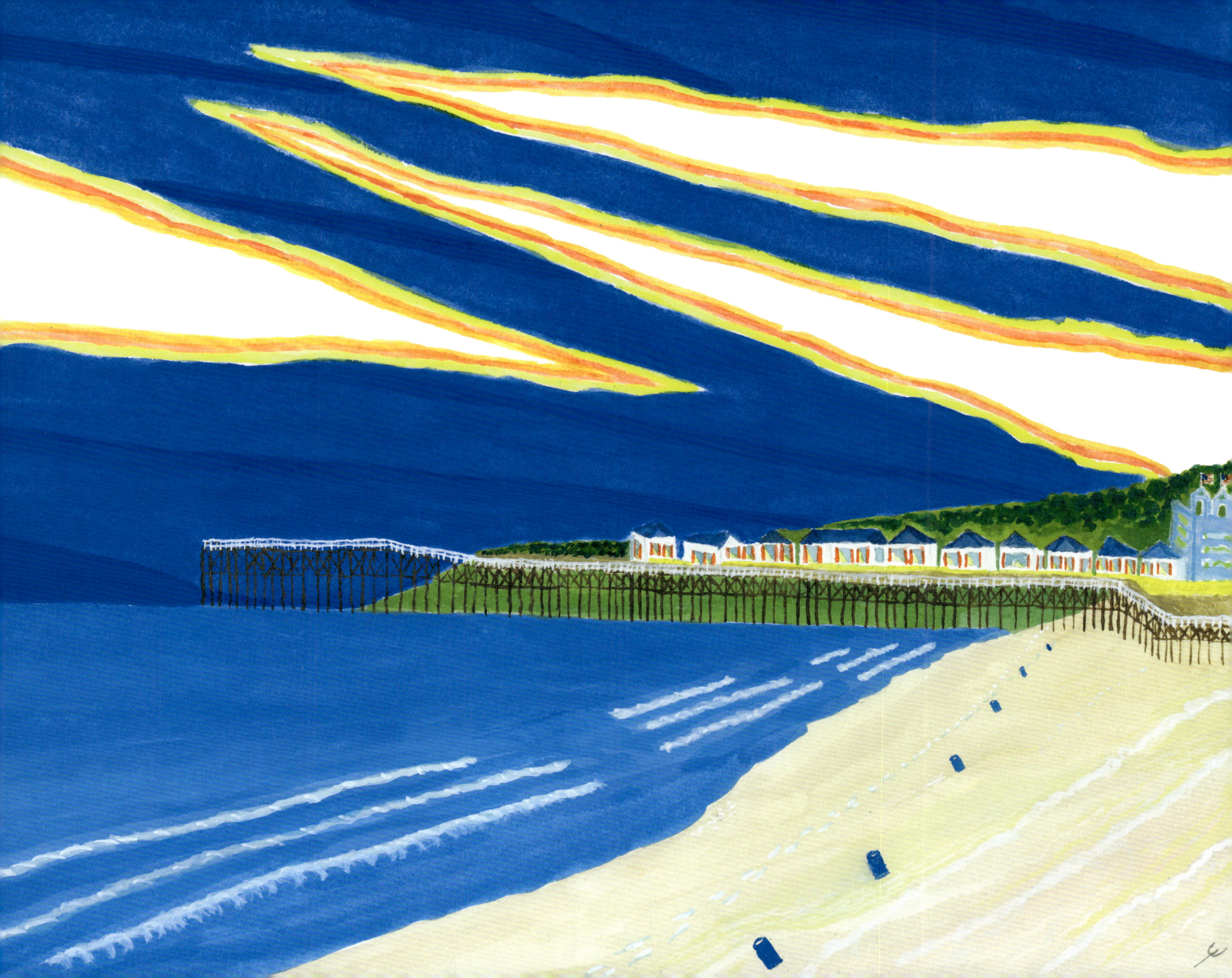

A Roundabout Way Home

A young man
and his toddler son
tumble
over and over,
as they roll
in the grass
on a sunny
hillside –
sky and earth,
earth and sky,
who can tell
one from the other,
when glimpsed
by a pair
of death-defying
acrobats?

A Faithful Suitor

Every evening
the amorous moonlight
paves
its silver road
across the ocean
to my windows,
and, stealing
down its own highway,
offers me
an elopement,
to a world
where waves
and islands
dance
all night
in their dreams.

Unimaginable Heights

A small bird,
fallen
from its nest,
flutters
across the grass,
until it reaches
a low shrub,
which extends
a branch
to the fledgling
who learns
flight's
first
hop.

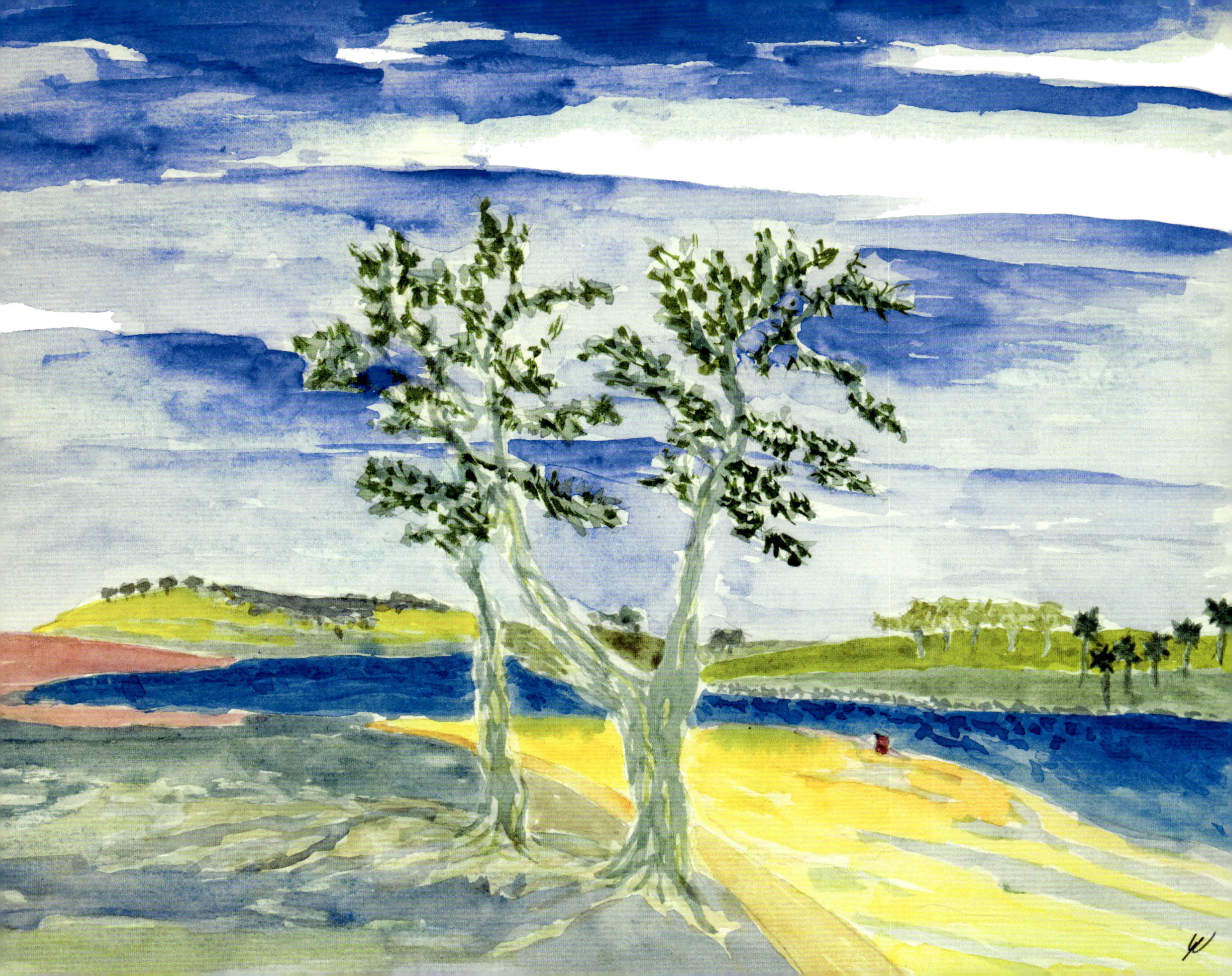

Reaching for the Heavens

A rocket
soars heavenward
on Christmas
at midnight –
not quite
a star,
it follows
its westward course,
illumining
for a moment
a beach,
where the land
and the ocean
give birth
to breakers,
to which the moon
bequeaths
a silver
crown.

Whooping It Up

A little boy,
singing
to himself
on Christmas Eve
day,
darts
around a building,
to hide
in a lair
of shadows,
then falls silent,
as he waits
for a playmate
to round
the corner,
unaware
that the tight-lipped
caroler
knows when
to tear open
his gift
of laughter.

New Faith

An old mission church,
red-roofed
and tan-faced,
waits
for a blue sky
to clear,
while the high clouds
and eucalyptus trees
line up
for their processional
behind the dusty sanctuary,
in which amber sunlight,
a zealous
convert,
tumbles through windows,
spilling
rainbows
onto the floor.

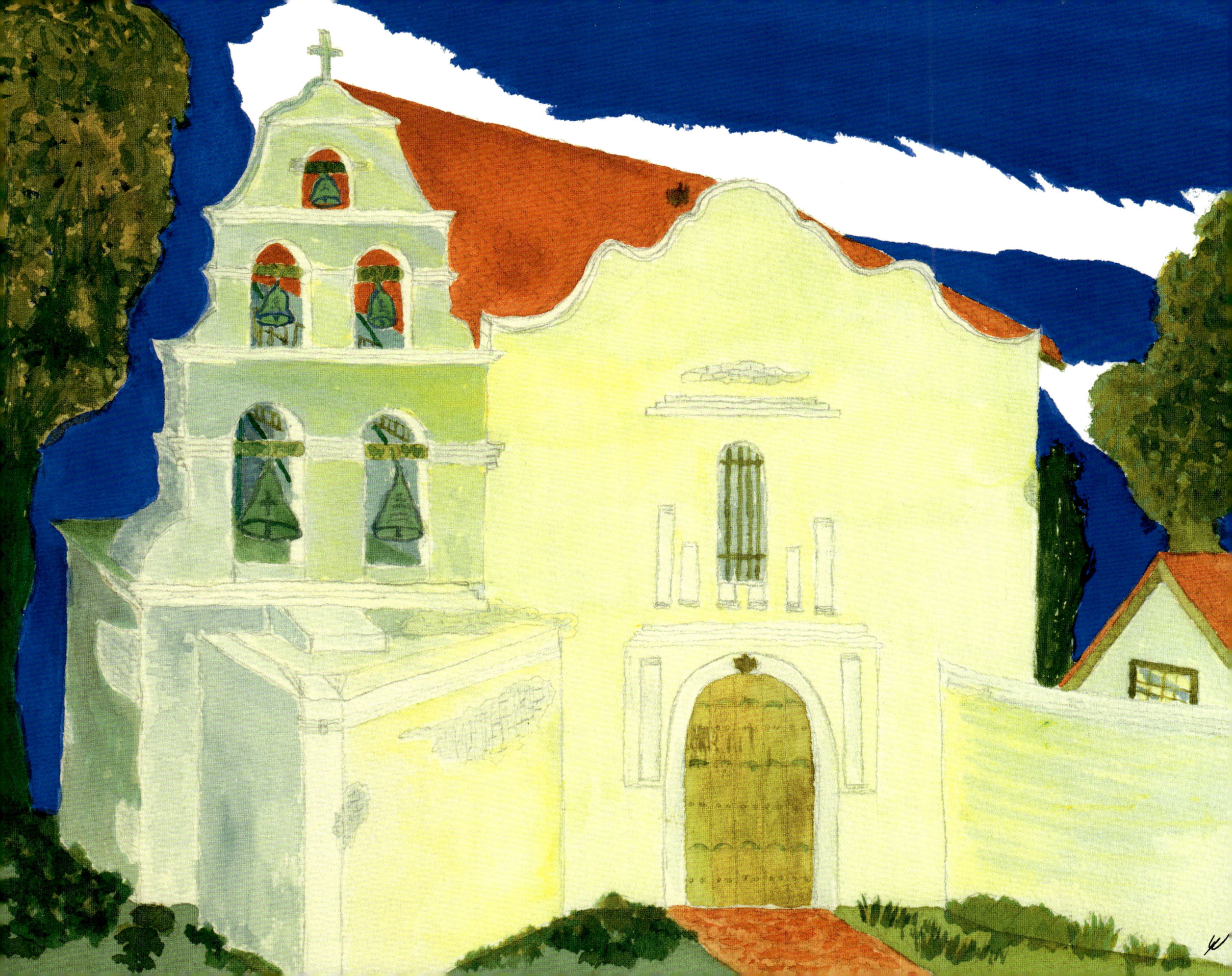

A Train of Thought

On a clear day,
I climb the highest hill,
to watch the still city
remember its past,
following fast
on the heels of tomorrow,
and the day before yesterday,
which never came home;
the buildings take shape
and abandon their names,
tossing their shadows
at the feet
of a peppery wind,
while parks sparkle green
and clouds use trapezes,
to get from old roofs
to a hole in the sky.

May Mysteries

A soap bubble,
floating
across an intersection,
captures
a host
of rainbows,
then drifts
into a garden,
where a petunia
is awakened
by a lemon-scented
shower
out of the blue.

Headed Home

The botanical building,
a railroad station
in another life,
now welcomes
bougainvillea
and gardenias
and cala lilies
and honeysuckle
and hydrangeas
and camelias,
distinguished travelers
that flourish
in different seasons,
and never ask
for an express ticket
to a distant soil.

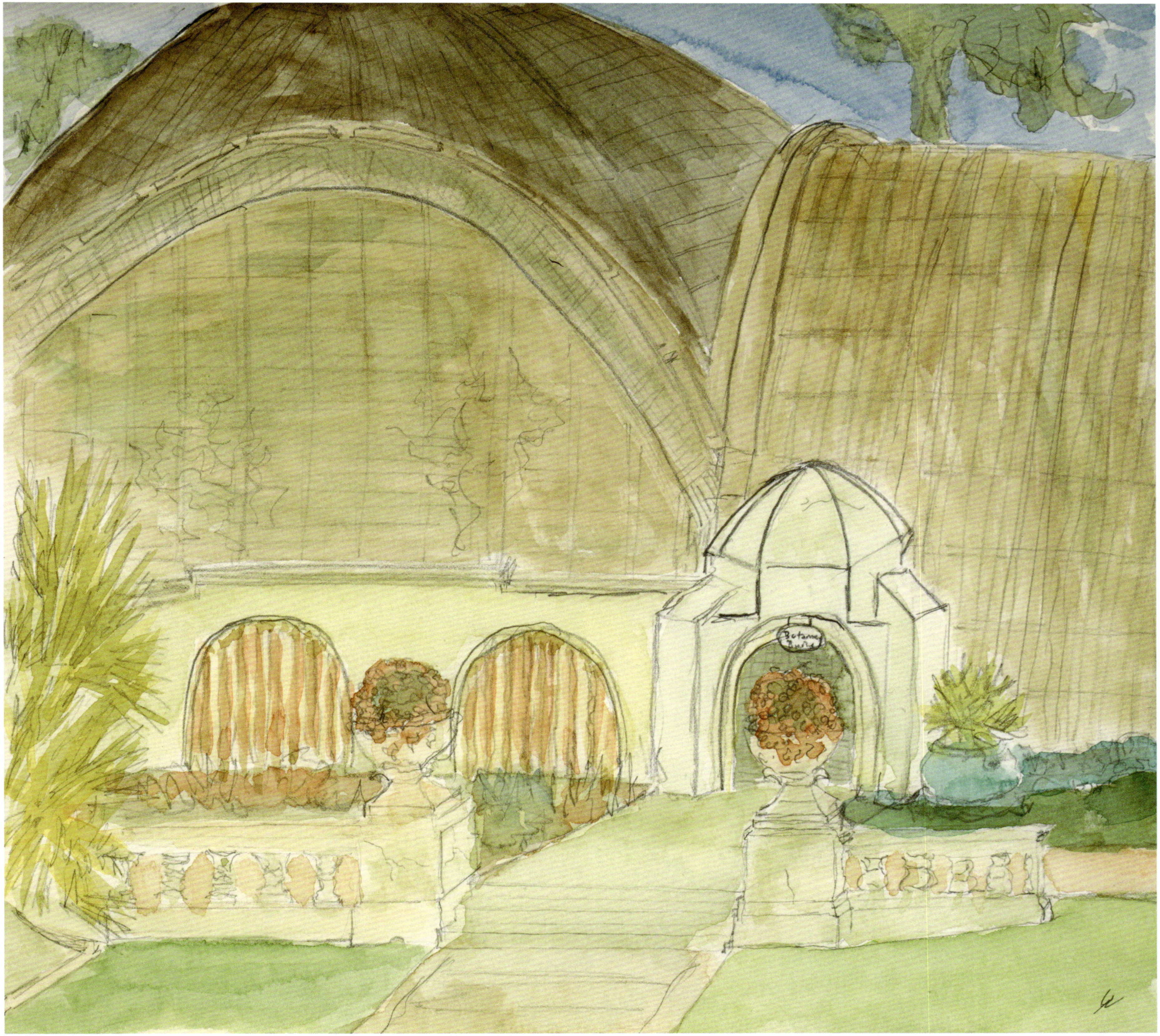

A Safe Place

Where is the happy valley,
the shelter
that does not
vanish?

Is there no place
where people bed down,
undaunted
by tomorrow's
uncertainties?

A middle-aged woman
smiles,
a toddler giggles
and runs to his mother,
an old man
warms himself
in sunlight
on a park bench,
and a dog, ambling
across a park,
sniffs at the breeze,
which has come chasing him
from the beginning
of time.

A January Scene

A young man
leans
over an old lady
in a wheelchair,
and whispers
a word or two
in a heartening
voice,
as the late afternoon sky
indulges
in an orange
and purple
smile.

Looking Inside and Out

The sky,
an orange smear
at sunset,
outstretches
its glow
from horizon to horizon,
raising its gaze
to a fading
blue pinnacle,
a wide-open
window,
where the sunlight
refuses
to stop
smiling.

Mission Bay and Belmont Park, San Diego

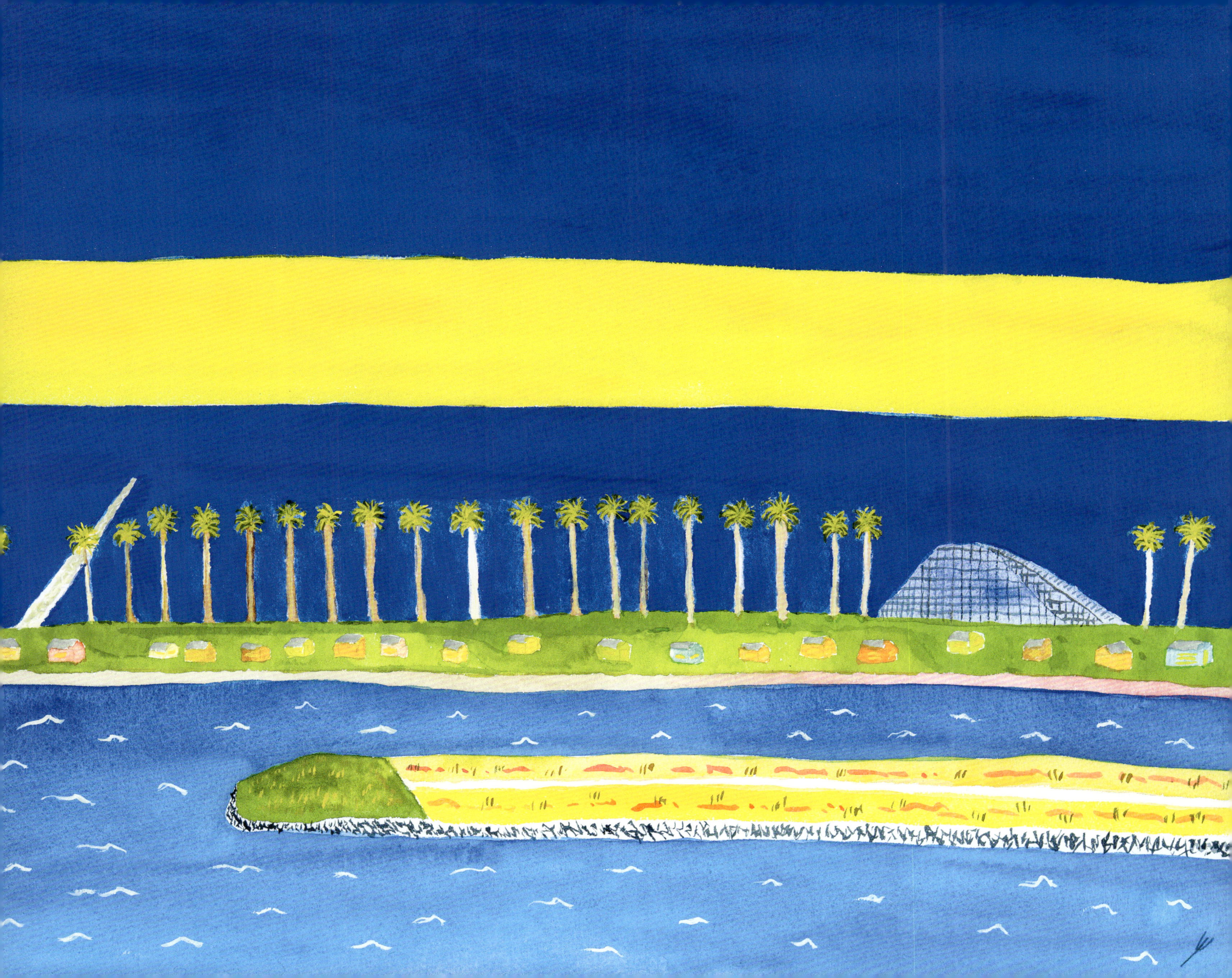

Making Do

A breeze
tugs
at palm fronds,
then releases
their fingertips –
soon another
will come calling,
they tell
one another,
and when it is gone,
they will
hold hands
in contentment,
wearing sunlight
for rings.

December Vigil

We stay up
at night
with sick children
and old people –
we know
that they answer
our prayers –
listening
to their hard-won
breath,
we touch their hands
and rub
their backs –
we are the lost ones,
they are our magi;
their fever
calms us
with memories
of winter skies,
in which the Milky Way
heals its wounds.

Wising Up

Golden light
on an old building
rests its soft hand
on an ornate
façade,
promising
no answers
to long-lived
mysteries,
only a smile
at an afternoon
sky.

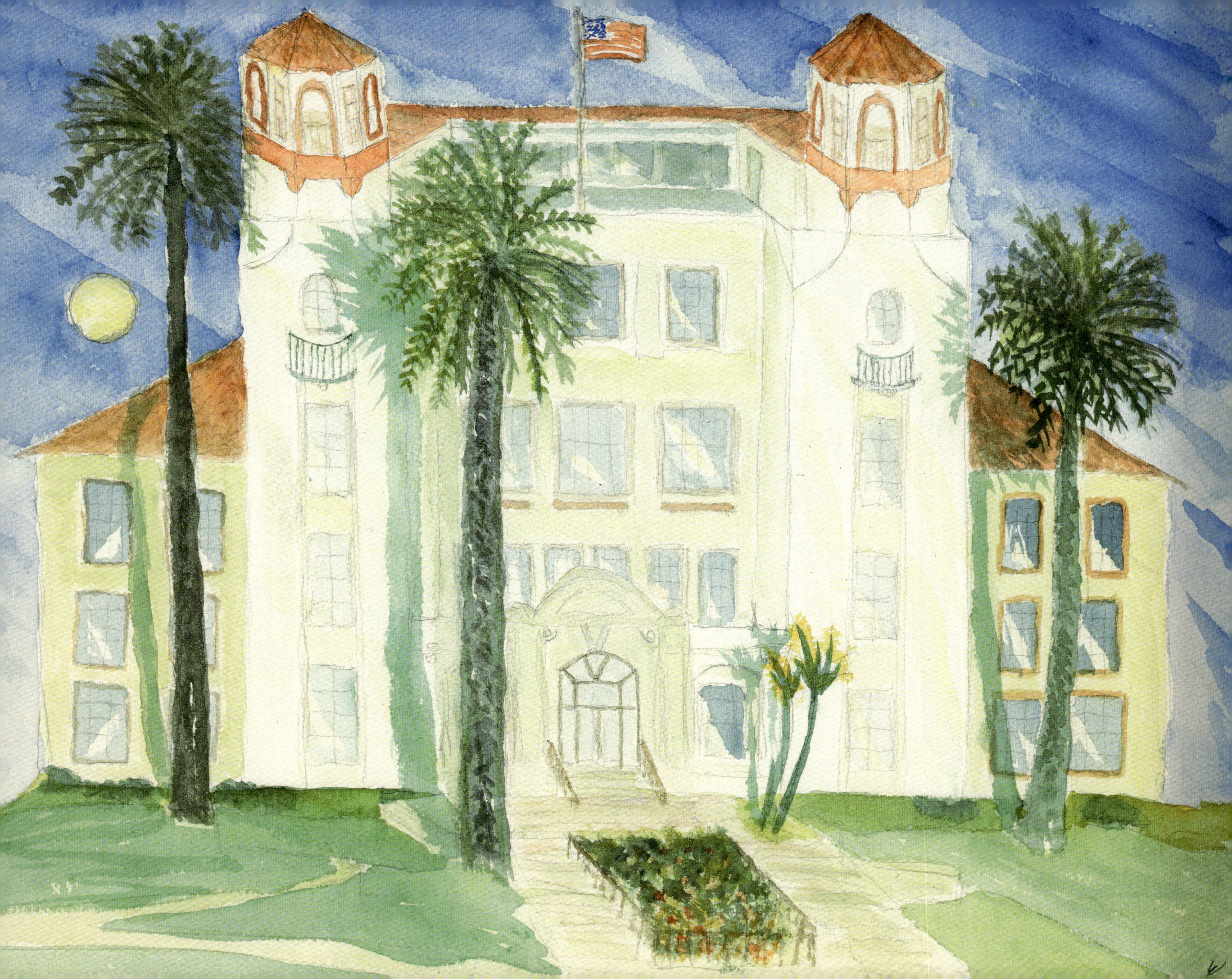

Young Love

Golden leaves
on a sapling
flutter
in the light blue sky,
showing off
their autumn finery,
their invitation
to a first dance,
on a day
when there are no wallflowers
in the breeze-enamored
forest.

Riding High

Falling
leaves
in rainbow
colors
scatter
and rise
in decorated
dustdevils,
decked out
for an autumn
sky,
so blue
that you wish it
a teary-eyed
cloud
for company.

High and Low

A canyon
in sunlight
and shadow
waits
on a hot day
for the sun
to pass
its apex,
then decline
behind clouds
that claim
to be
the first cousins
of mountains.

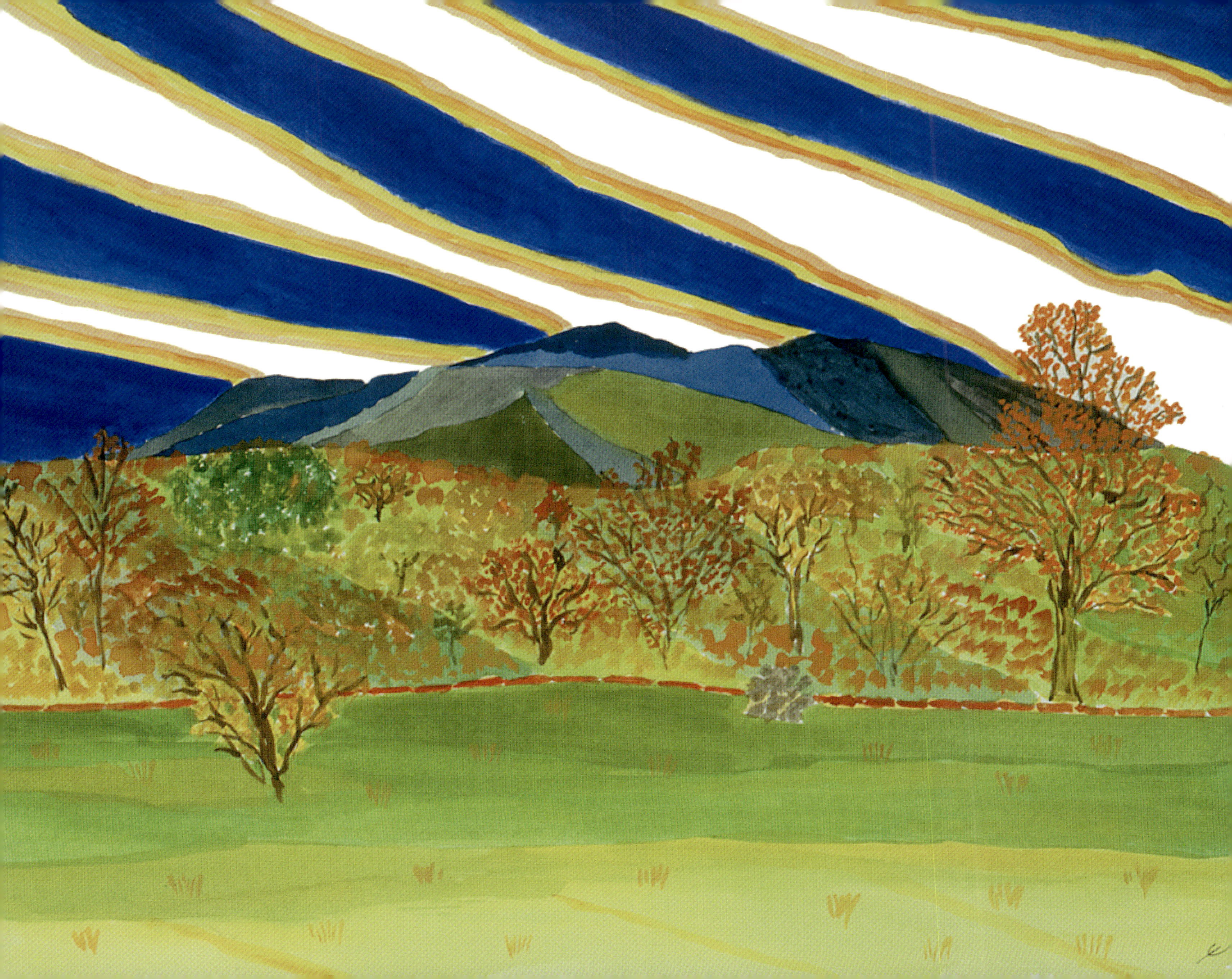

Garden Whispers

A quiet morning
under the fog
unfurls
its lily petals,
inviting the ocean
to blossom
in secret,
to offer
its field of hydrangeas
to a sun
as shy
as a white rose
in moonlight.

The Little Bang

A clear-eyed day
beside the ocean
glitters
from horizon to horizon –
from mountains
to waves,
the light
dances
to the universe's
laughter,
then sets out
for a shore
where shadows
mark the time
by pointing
in every direction.

Setting Out

For a moment,
the light
smiles
on a hilltop,
or from the face
of a tumbledown
wall,
or in the middle
of a twisting
path,
and you remember
the promise
of a day
that awakens
early,
to make its way
out of a canyon
to scale a promontory,
where eternity
comes down
to this –
one glance
in every direction,
then a bold
step
upon the road.

Pt. Loma

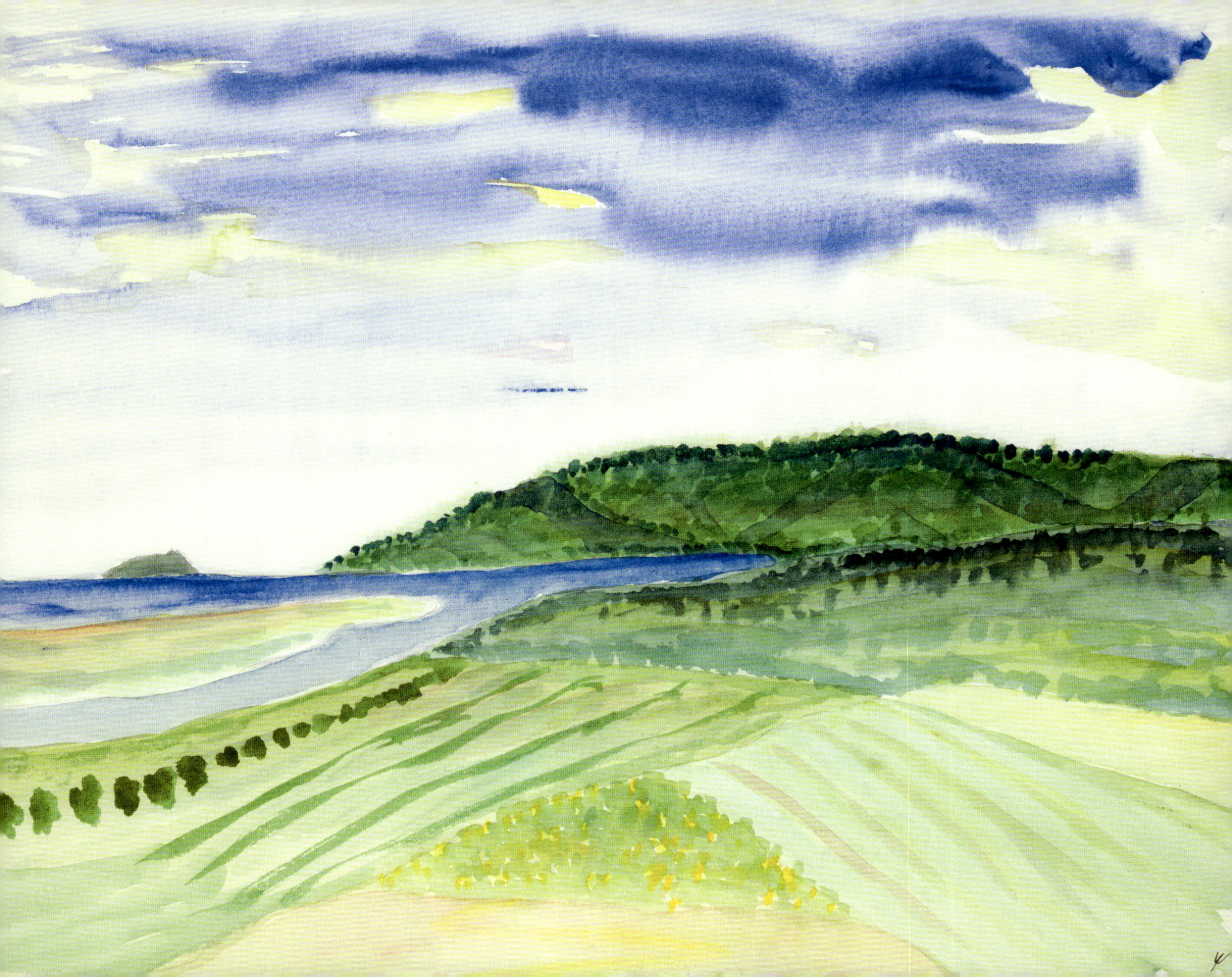

Kind Embraces

A calm day
beside the coast
gives the ocean
and the land
a chance
to gaze
at one another,
as the sky
clears,
and the waves
turn over
in their sleep,
and the clouds
bask
in early light,
while a sailboat
dances
with every breeze
that ambles
its way.

Long Shots

An empty
boat
bobs
in the harbor –
the sunlight
dapples it
and moves on,
riding the backs
of waves
that somersault
onto beaches
that slap
their thighs
and laugh.

At Anchor

A solitary sailboat,
stirring
at its mooring,
turns
toward the ocean,
then murmurs
to waves
that its furled sails
are itching.

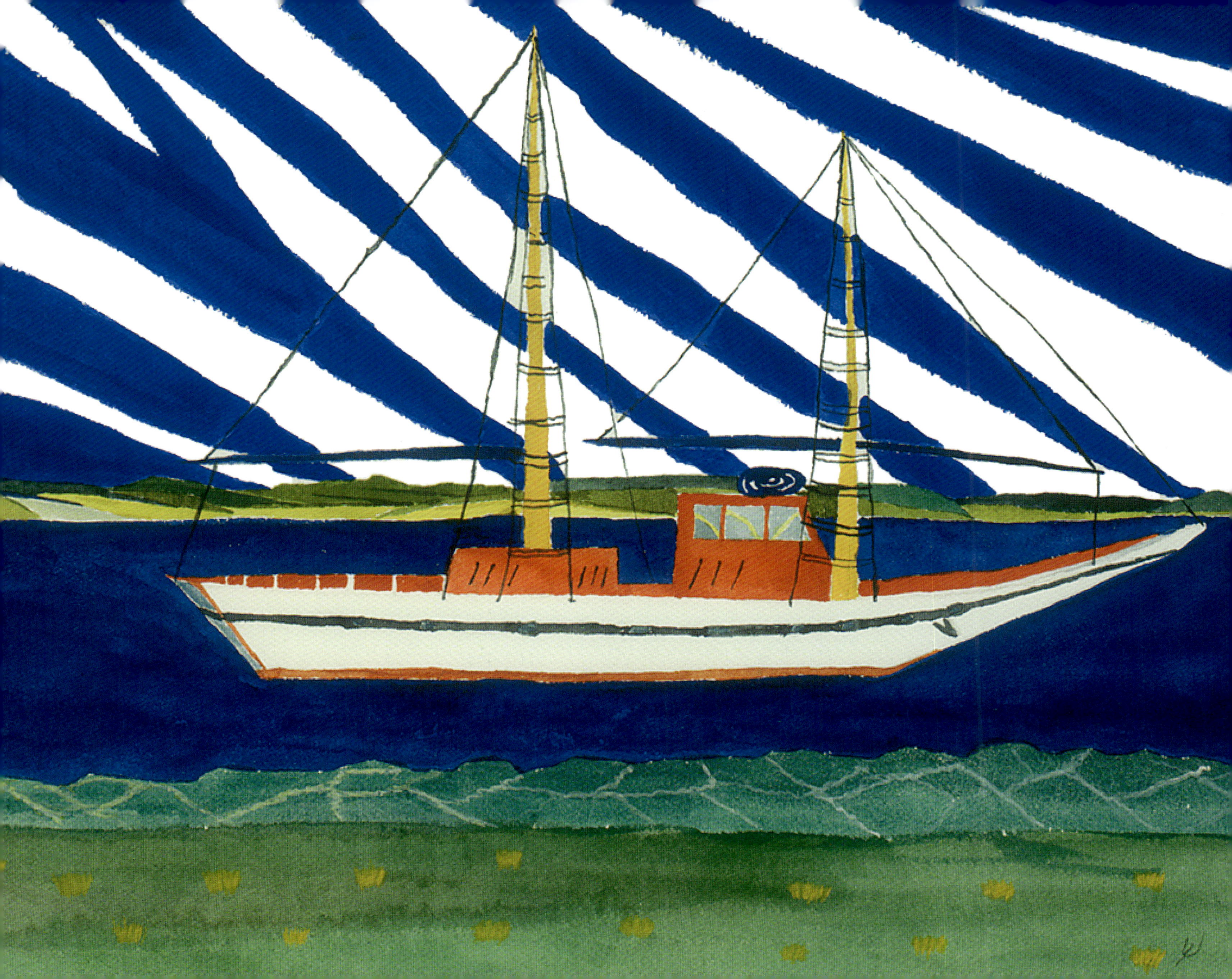

Helping Hands

Delicate
palm fronds,
swayed
by the wind,
make friends
with their own
timid shadows,
which sweep clean
a sidewalk
to make room
for sunlight.

Taking Stock

A black caterpiller
inches his way
across a sleepy
asphalt street –
what an act
of death-defying
grace,
by a soft-coated
sojourner
who may
or may not
win his
angel's
wings.

In a green
arbor
across the way,
a patch
of soft grass
unfurls
paradise.

Celebrating Summer

A bright day
beside the ocean
glistens
under a calm-eyed
sky –
July heat
beckons
from morning on,
while the waves
dance
on tiptoe,
in the arms
of lighthearted
breezes.

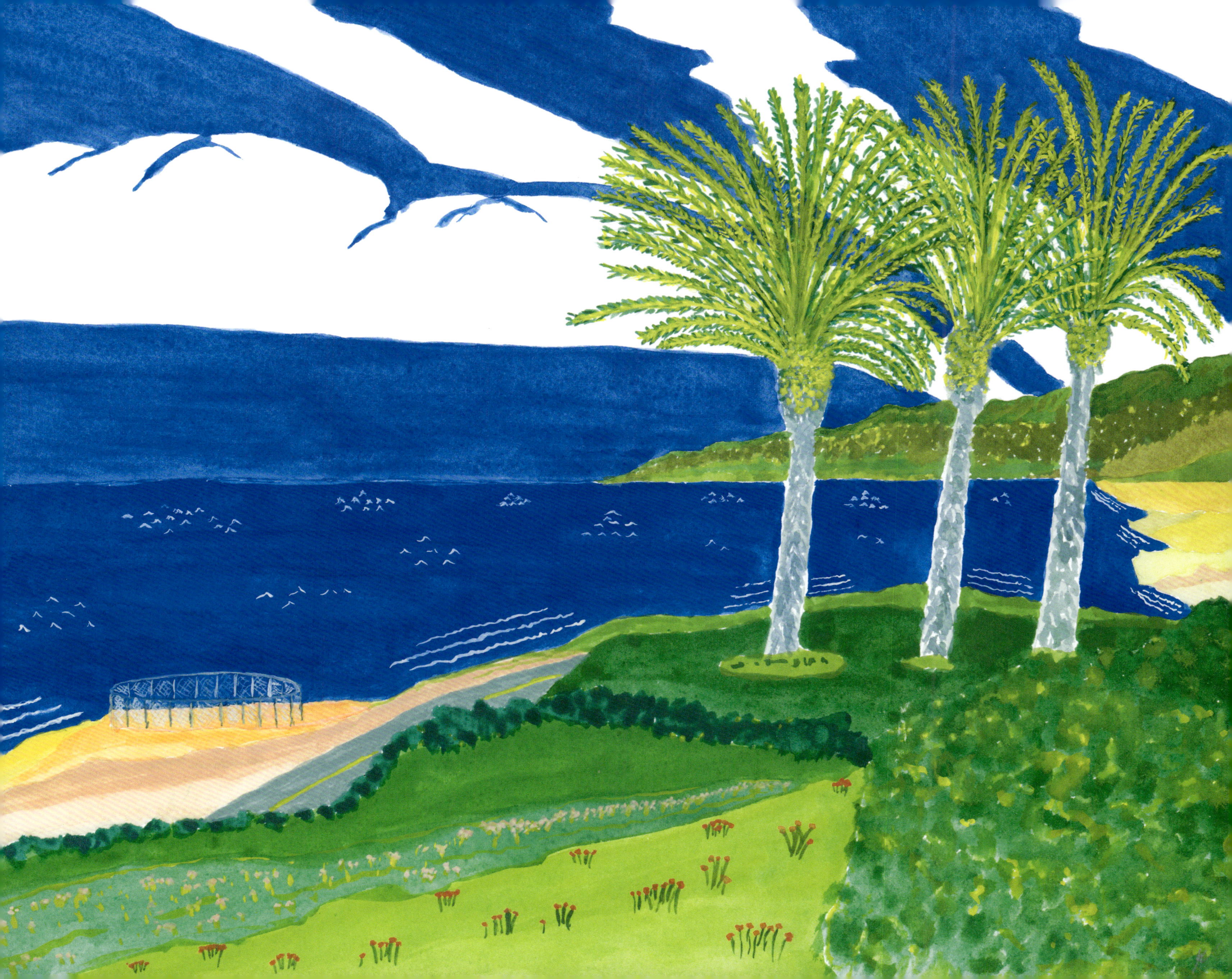

A Bright-Eyed Flirtation

A rainbow
dances
before you,
following
the land
as you jog down
a path –
leaping
from hill to hill,
it cavorts
out to sea,
then promises
to spill its colors
from reef
to mountain.

You cannot
catch it –
the land
is its dance partner,
but watching it
flit ahead,
you wink
at the sky.

Looking Up

A rainbow
over the ocean
holds together
two lakes
of gray
with a multi-colored
bridge,
walking on water
for the fun of it.

A Blithe Truant

Late light,
orange
and lavender
and yellow
and pink
and mauve
and teal,
wallows
on the horizon,
like a rainbow
that has overeaten
and fallen
on soft times.

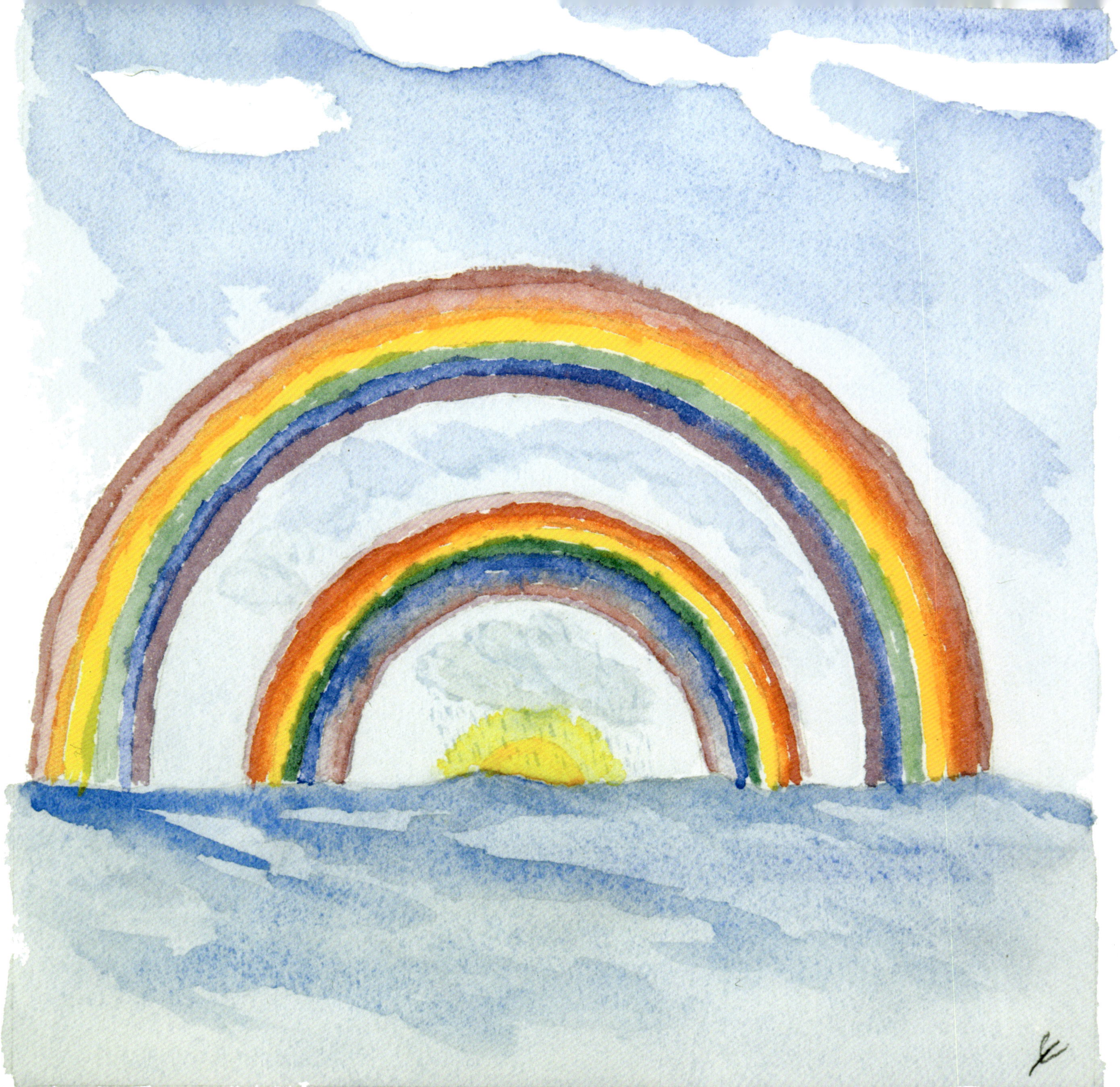

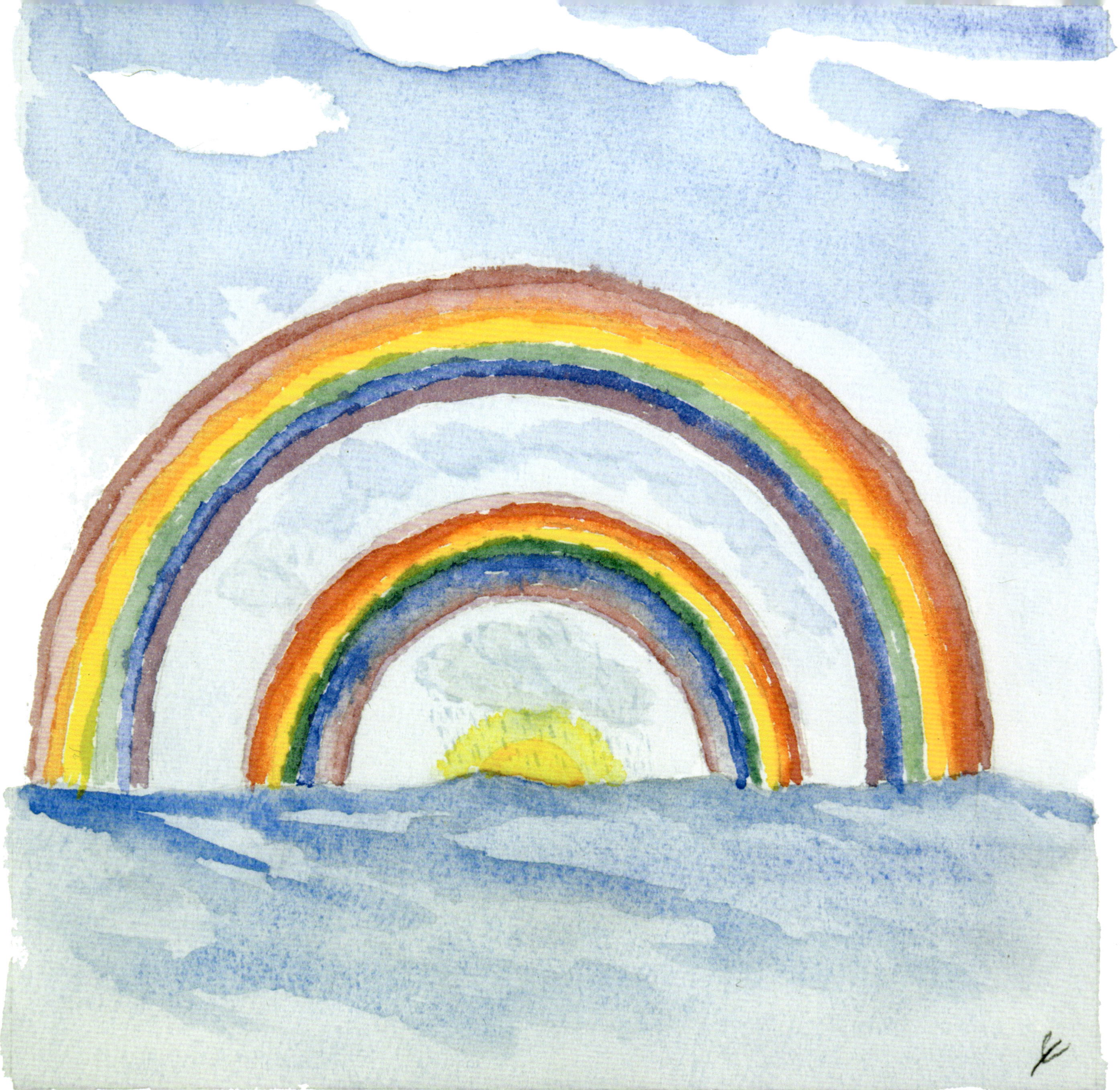

Daredevil

An old gentleman,
setting forth
on a walk
at dusk,
follows
the setting sun
down the street,
only to kick up his heels
at the sight
of the first traffic signal,
winking
its red
and green
eyes,
in an instant
when it blinks
its yellow invitation
to throw caution
to the wind.

Trolling the Line

A middle-aged man
sits
with his son,
waiting
for a judge
to deal
with their problem.

In the same
white business shirts,
they lean back
and fall silent,
daydreaming
of fishing,
and a sky
that is turning blue
outside a straight
and narrow
window.

One Dancer

"The Noblest
Motive
Is the Public
Good,"
exhorts
the inscription
above the county building's
portal,
while its blunt-browed
façade
reflects
brilliant
sunlight,
as it beams
across the harbor
at a solitary
skiff,
for which the waves
have made room.

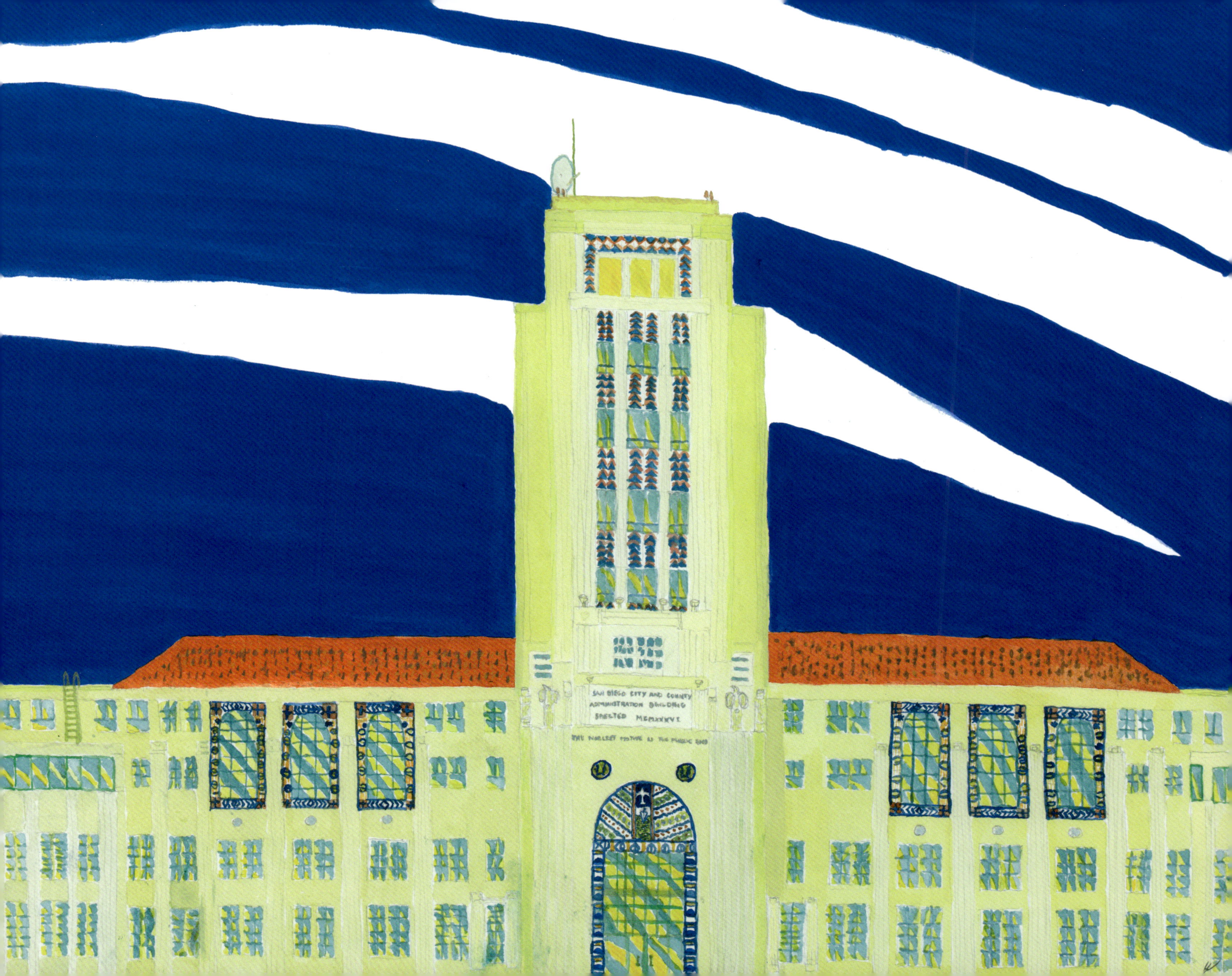
CITY AND
ADMINISTRATION

California Humor

A quiet city,
chuckling
at dawn,
awakens
to the sounds
of its laughter,
to the tittering
of sheepish breezes,
and the ocean's
drunken
guffaw.

Conversation

We talk
about Eastern
and Western
philosophies,
and certainty
and uncertainty,
and the meanings
of our birth signs;
and when lunch
is over,
and the table
has been cleared,
there still is the matter
of washing the dishes,
with warm water
and suds,
welcome partners
with no opinions
except about the kindness
of the Water Department.

Brave Enough

Palm trees
in the fog,
gray-bearded
sentinels,
stand guard
along the coast,
watching the waves
as they tumble
to the coast,
while the palms
doze off
at their posts,
content to wait
for a freshening wind
to tap them
on the shoulders,
and a blue sky
to decorate them
for their daydreams
of valor.

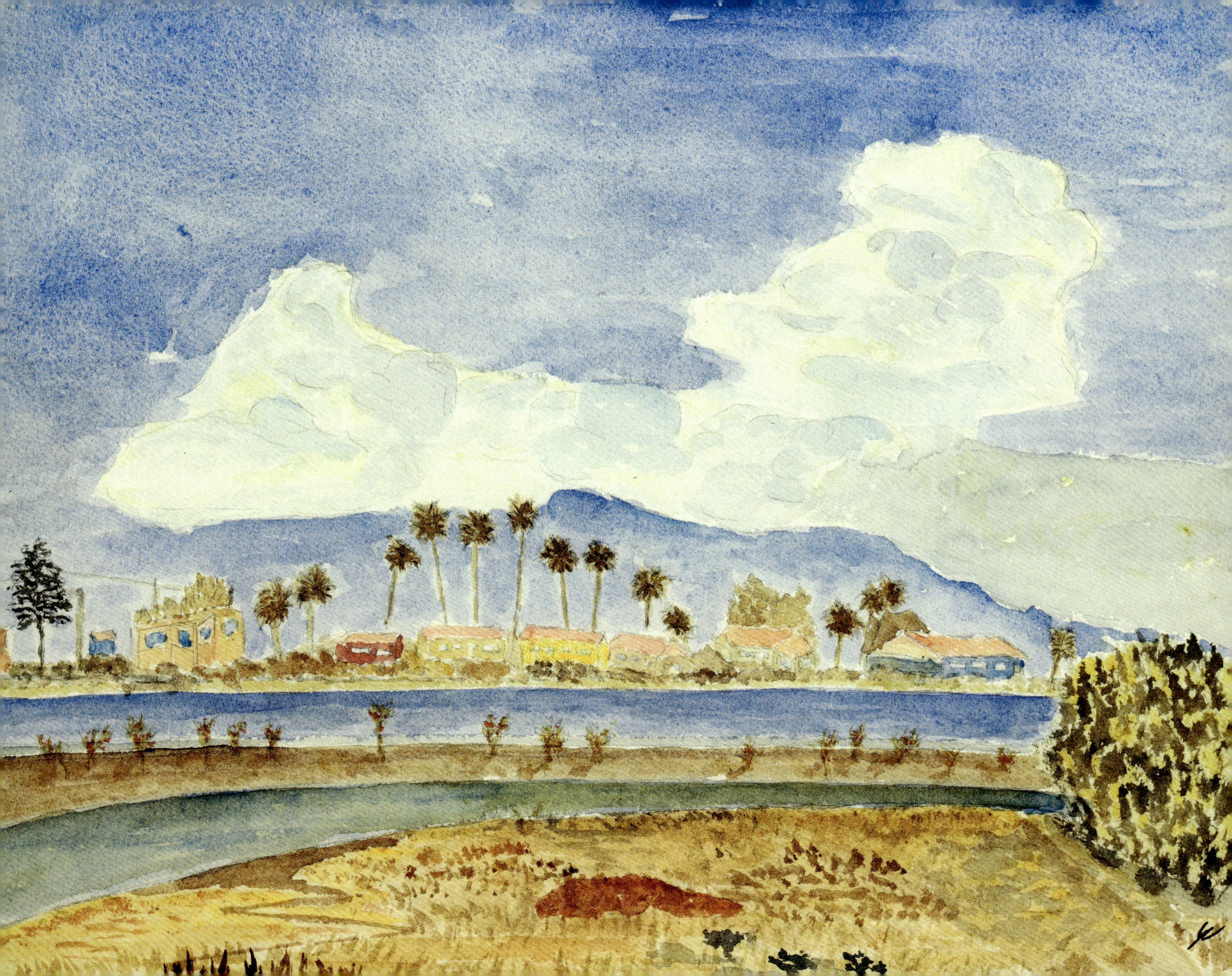

California Property

Mountains
and ocean
bask
in the sunlight,
while beyond them,
the desert
sells mirages
cheap.

Bright Coiffure

A gray-haired
lady
sits reading
beside the bay,
as she gazes out
at its furrowed brow;
with her short hair
and slender
smile,
she reassures
the waves
that they will make good
on their promise
to get home
on time,
leaving the fog
to let down
its hair
in afternoon
sunlight.

Bright Virtues

The mountains,
all gray and blue
above the morning mist,
welcome
the haloes
that first light
bestows
on them,
whether
they are
high-principled
or
simply
tall daydreamers.

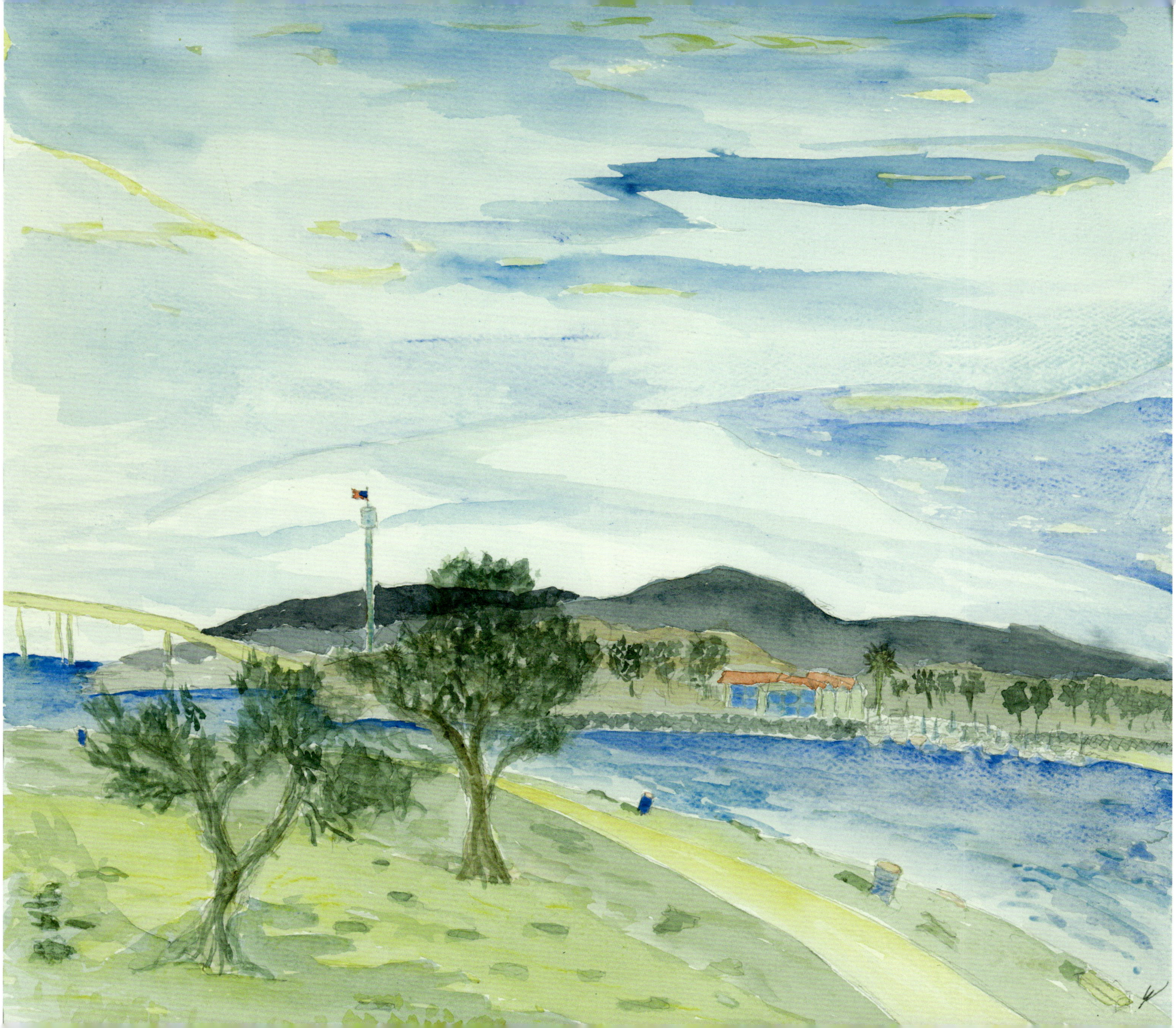

Heading West

The happy valley,
awaited
for so many years,
opens its lap
to the sunlight,
and to wayfarers
who have found it,
nestled
between the last mountains
and the first ocean.

High Life

Five palm trees
and a flock
of clouds
offer the blue sky
a final gift
on Thanksgiving,
a moment's
silence,
reaching
upward
to hold its breath.

Acrobatics

The ocean
mulls over
a sunny day,
and turns cartwheels
as it greets
the shore –
slapping the hips
of the amber beach,
it trumpets
and hoots
and sputters,
before turning
a back flip
into the arms
of its own
roly-poly
waves.

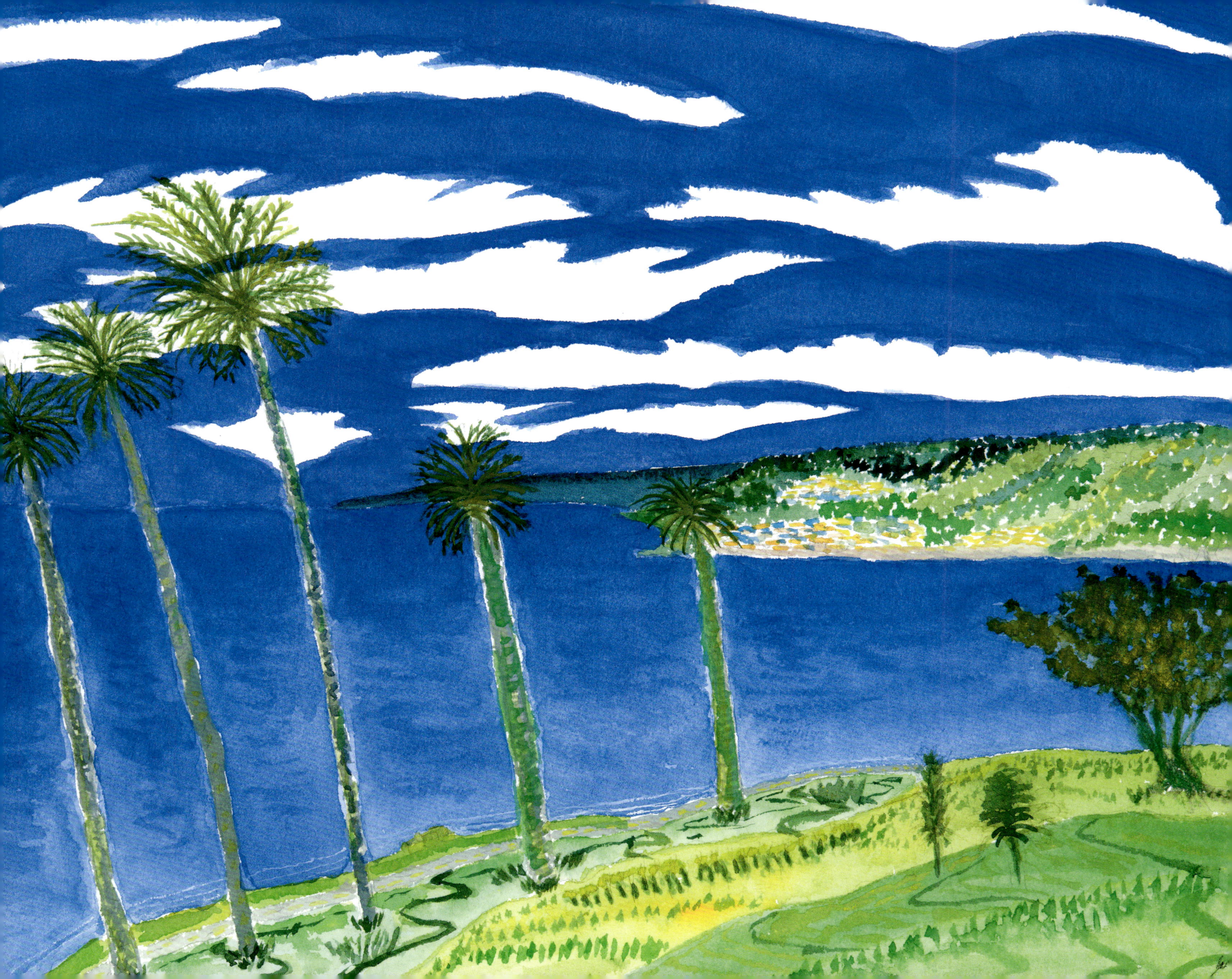

Faith

On Good Friday,
you chronicle
a new prayer –
Lord,
give me
gentler eyes
with which
to greet
my brothers
and sisters.

Lord,
give me time
to recognize them
everywhere.

An Unsung Serenade

Three musicians
in a cantina,
playing
under honeyed light,
look up
from their guitar,
accordion,
and harmonica,
with glances
of surprise –
someone
has walked in,
and their song
saddens
the stars
that the open door
caresses.

Father Serra's Daydream

Martyrs
and missionaries
and Tipai
and Ipai
and Luiseño
and Gabrielino
and Chumash
and Salinan
and Esselen
and Coastanoan
and Coast Miwok
and Pomo
share their memories
of the land –
of clay-red adobe,
plastered white,
and crosses
above dusty courtyards,
and beyond them
the fields,
squared and planted,
where once
there were only
untamed grasses.

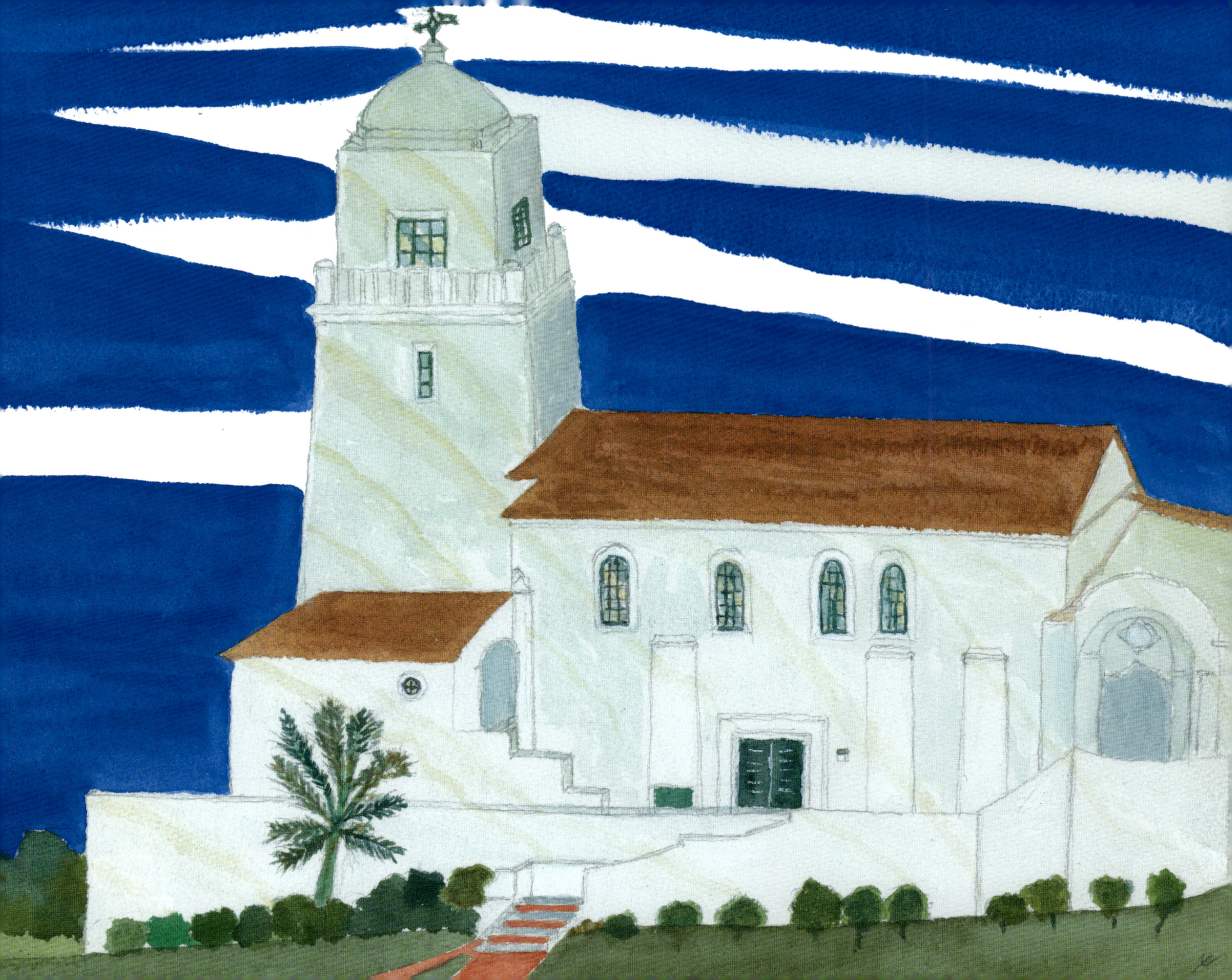

A Spring Shower

Storm clouds
over the ocean
unfurl
their gray
parasols,
sheltering
the waves
from a downpour
of sunlight,
which startles
the water
with a brilliant-eyed
glance.

Seeing Inside

The ocean,
a dappled mirror,
reflects
the high clouds,
dancing
with graceful breezes –
flattered
by the silver glass,
the clouds
drift apart,
then discover
that the ocean
has its own depths
to admire.

A Quiet Swell

Winter light
at the hem
of the ocean
holds the purple waves
to their promise –
to settle down
after the gray storms
have passed,
and keep house
with the bright-eyed
horizon.

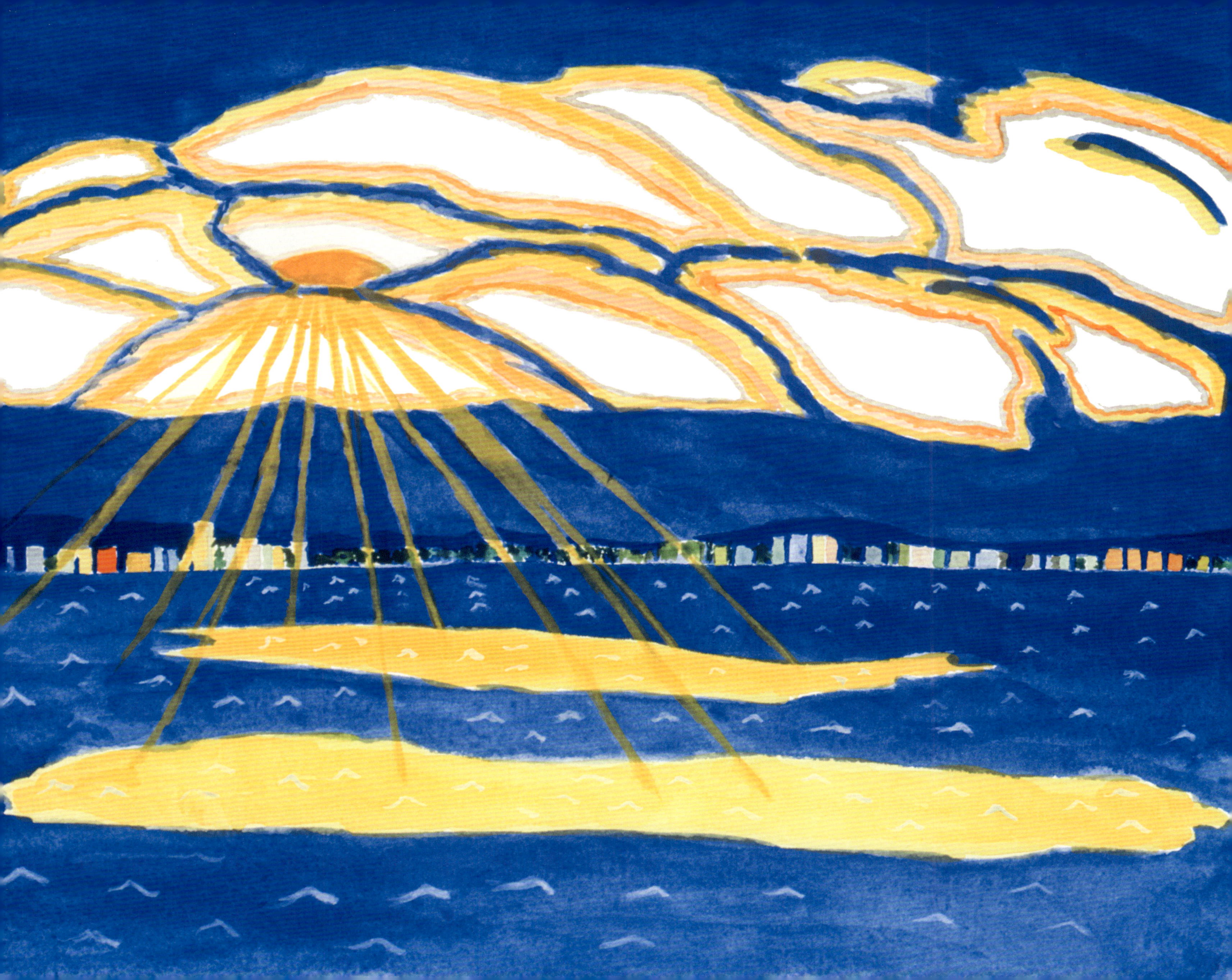

An Early Homecoming

An open harbor
spreads wide
its arms,
inviting strangers
to sail in
with the sunlight –
sparkling
in morning light,
the waves
hug the shore,
then whisper
of distant ports,
where clouds
weep with joy
at the sight
of green
mountains.

Pleasant Surprises

Blue mountains
before a yellow sky
at dawn
raise
their sentinel
flags,
their signal
pennants
that promise
a day
of homecoming,
a day
when the sunlight
will bed down
with gardens
that blossom
in autumn.

New Life

The ocean,
reborn
day after day,
opens
its waves
to the caress
of sunny shores,
which kneel down
to touch
breakers
that have risen
from the deep,
to murmur
in their cradles
of sand.

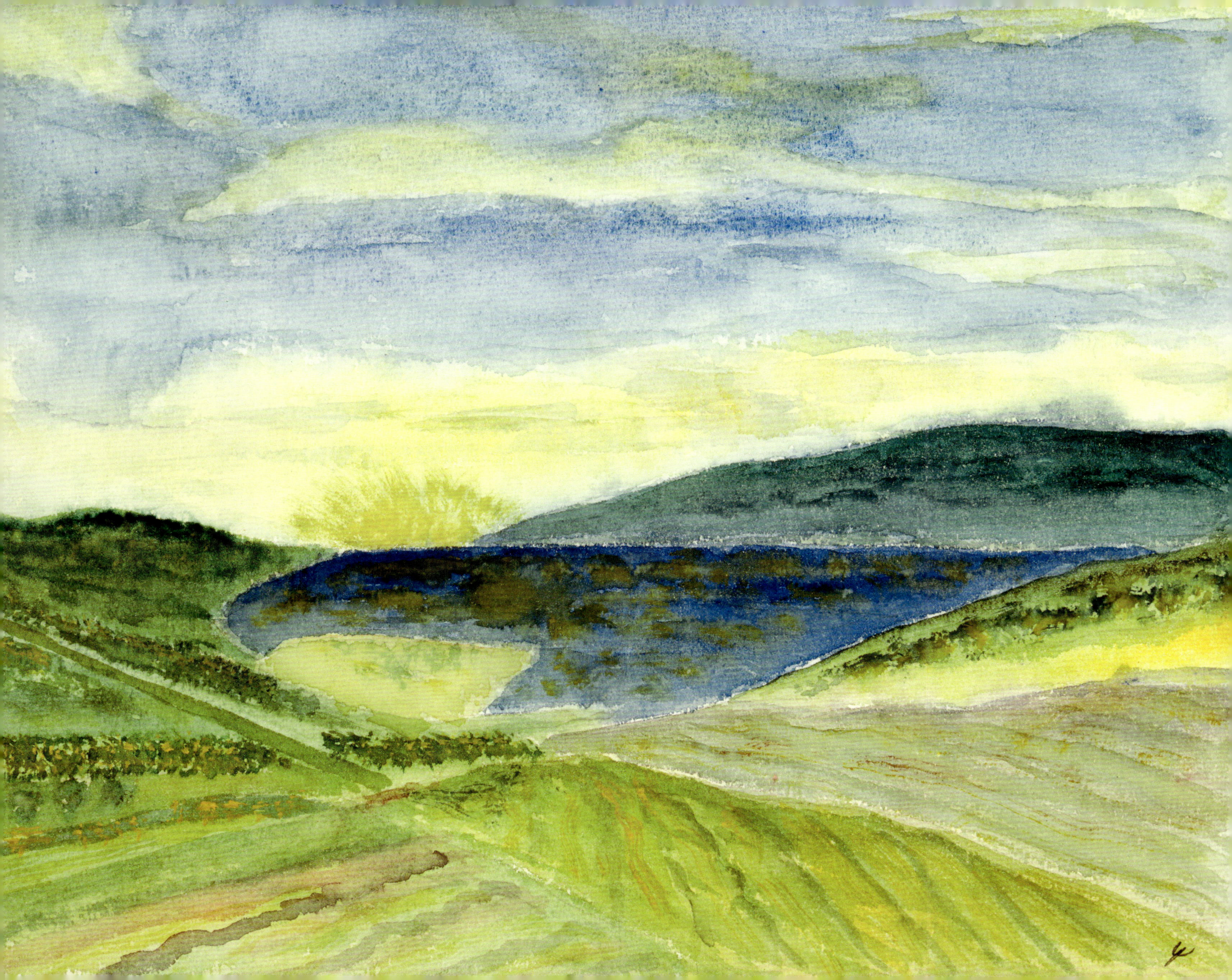

Fantastic Partners

Light
on the hem
of the ocean,
bobbing
among skirts
of foam,
takes a whirl
with every incoming wave
that struts its way
onto the beach's
waxed
dance floor.

A Question of Faith

The cynical man
at the beach,
the bald, pot-bellied man
who does not smile
at anyone –
not even
at his children,
as they cavort
among the waves –
frowns
at broad-shouldered surfers
and laughter-squandering
lovers
and wave-tagging
runners
and volleyball players
who dance
in mid-air;
until, scowling down
at his crumpled
soda can,
he stands up
to struggle
against a tide of sand,
to reach a gray-bearded man
who collects the cans
in a garbage can
that drools
beer –
"If you'd take this can,
I'd be much obliged,"
he drawls
to the stranger,
who smiles
at a brother
who has spoken up bravely,
above the gray
ocean's
roar.

Taming Breakers

Surfers
climb
onto their dream boards,
parting
the white beards
of waves,
as the late sun
tints
the clouds
red and gold,
and the sky
rides piggyback
on the ocean's
broad shoulders.

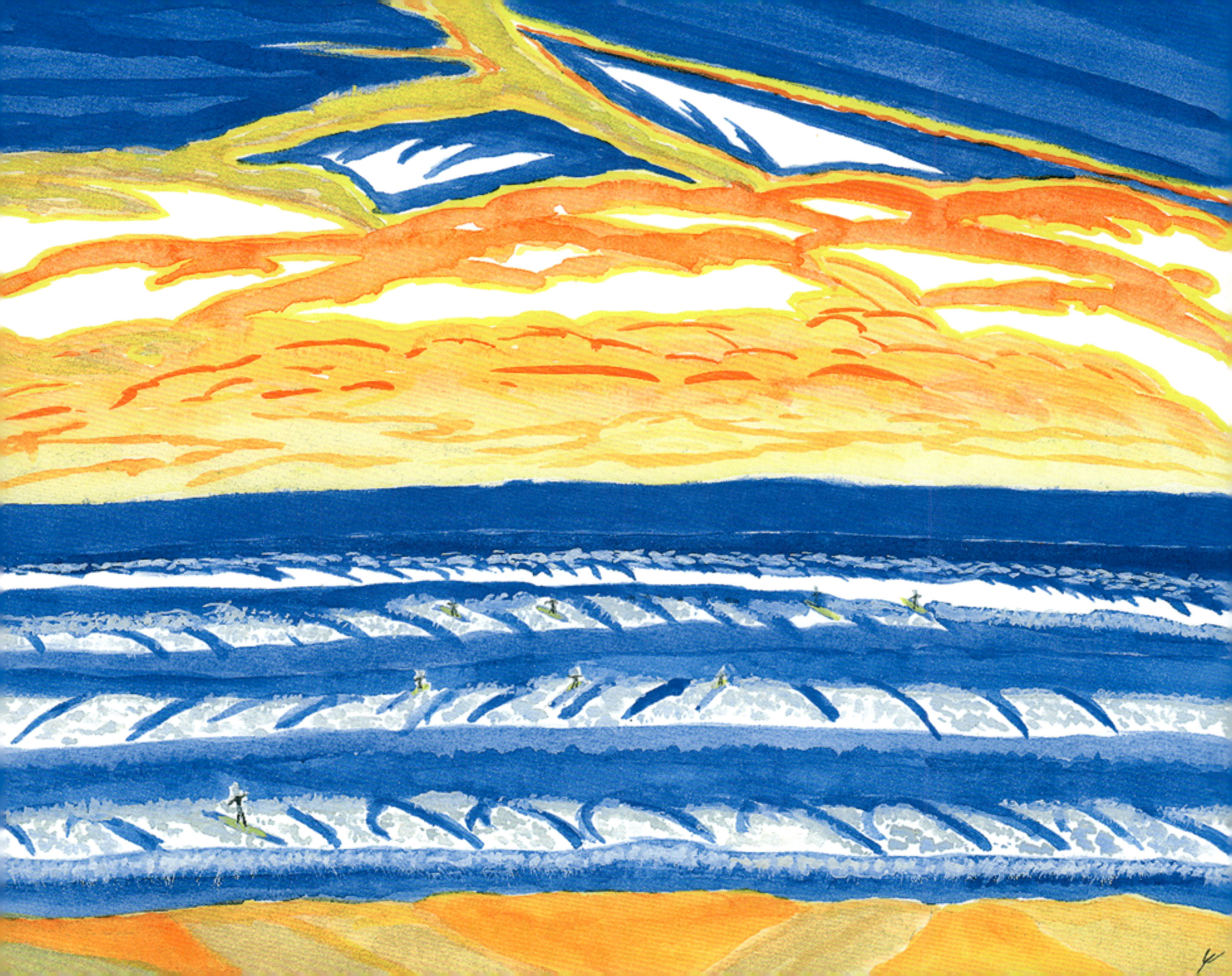

Winter Promises

Distant stars,
hung in the sky,
promise
a life
above the horizon,
a cluster
of fireflies
that do not tire
of setting out
their beacons.

Bright Gifts

A middle-aged man,
lonely
on a sunny Thanksgiving
afternoon,
asks me the time,
as I sit painting
in the park;
and when I explain
that I do not
have a watch,
he asks
a woman
who is walking,
and who offers
the stranger
half
of a smile,
before she strides on,
leaving him
to turn to me
and tell me
that it's almost four
o'clock,
just in case
I need
reminding
that the winter
sunlight
has not much longer
to lavish itself
on my canvas.

Spring Tidings

Tropical shadows
intertwine
on a path
to the ocean,
while boughs
cast down
their shifting nets,
catching
sunlight,
as it warms
a trail
that meanders
into the lap
of an open-armed
beach.

And still
the waves,
silver-crested,
daydream
of gardens
that doze
within earshot
of thundering
breakers.

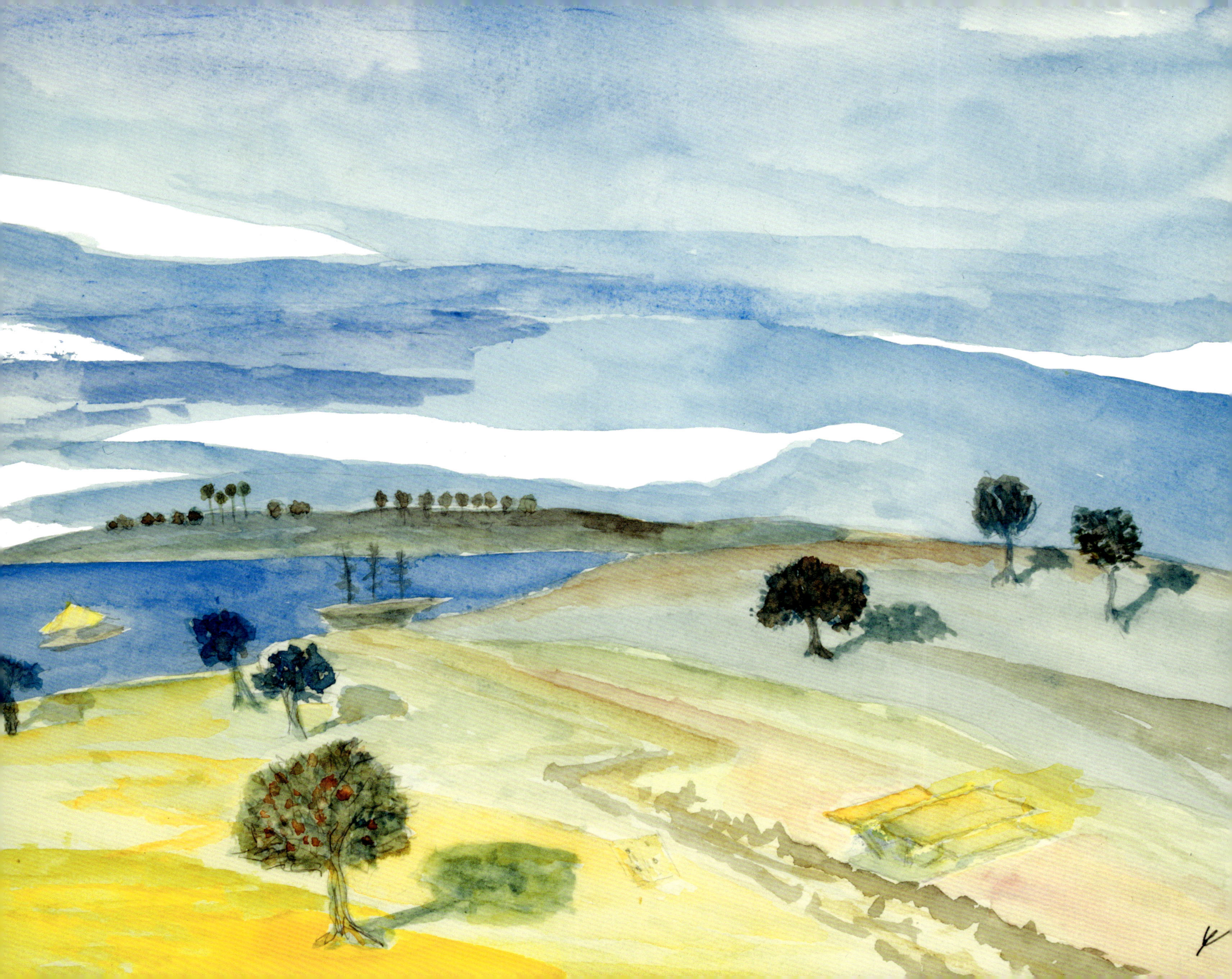

Prometheus Unbound

A distant headland
lies in sunlight,
while waves
tumble about it,
and the green hills
climb down
to the sea
on hands and knees,
and the horizon,
glistening
under clearing skies,
smiles
at a promontory
that points
to the ends
of the earth,
where islands
and continents
scatter their shadows
upon the waves,
confident
that they will find
their way home,
while a headland
reaches out
to the headstrong
ocean,
and draws back
in its hand
a bouquet of fireflies.

Minds of Their Own

Sitting in the sun
on the last autumn day,
you turn over the horizon
and count on your toes:
more than one godsend,
more than one grief –
all to be gathered up
and lent to the road –
without chasing off
the thin time of day,
you have made its stout shadow
saunter away,
saving your pilgrimage
for a day
in the fall,
when you put on your borrowed shoes
and kick up
spring dust.

Sunny Beginnings

Golden light
at the horizon,
light
over the ocean,
after an endless
journey,
settles down
to welcome you home,
just when you thought
that the west
had given up
on lighting
a bonfire.

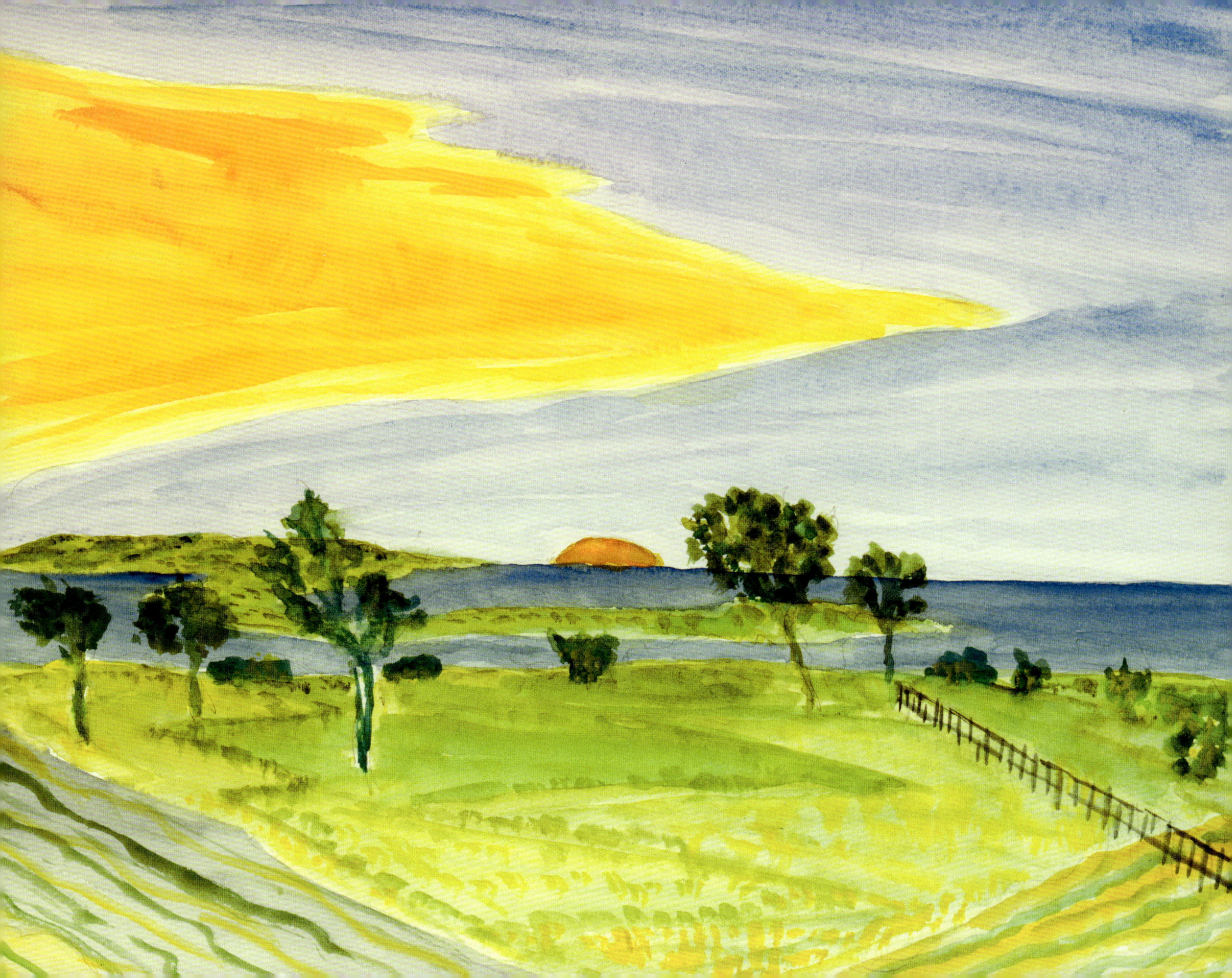

Midsummer

The dawn,
coming
early,
reveals
a calm ocean
that has kicked off
its coverlet
of clouds.

Waves
hold hands
in the newborn
light,
and coastlines
sing out,
to be discovered
by a westering
sun.

Getting Here

The ocean,
aglitter
on a perfect day,
opens its lap
to the weary
and the wise-eyed –
with no fear,
it buoys
itself up,
and laps
the shore
with the calm
of a long-distance
swimmer.

Harboring Hope

Light
on the distant
ocean,
light
beyond the shadows
of the farthest
clouds,
waits
for a sailboat
to ride
into its bright river;
and if none
appears
in the soft afternoon,
it will settle
for lending
the horizon
a tardy
smile.

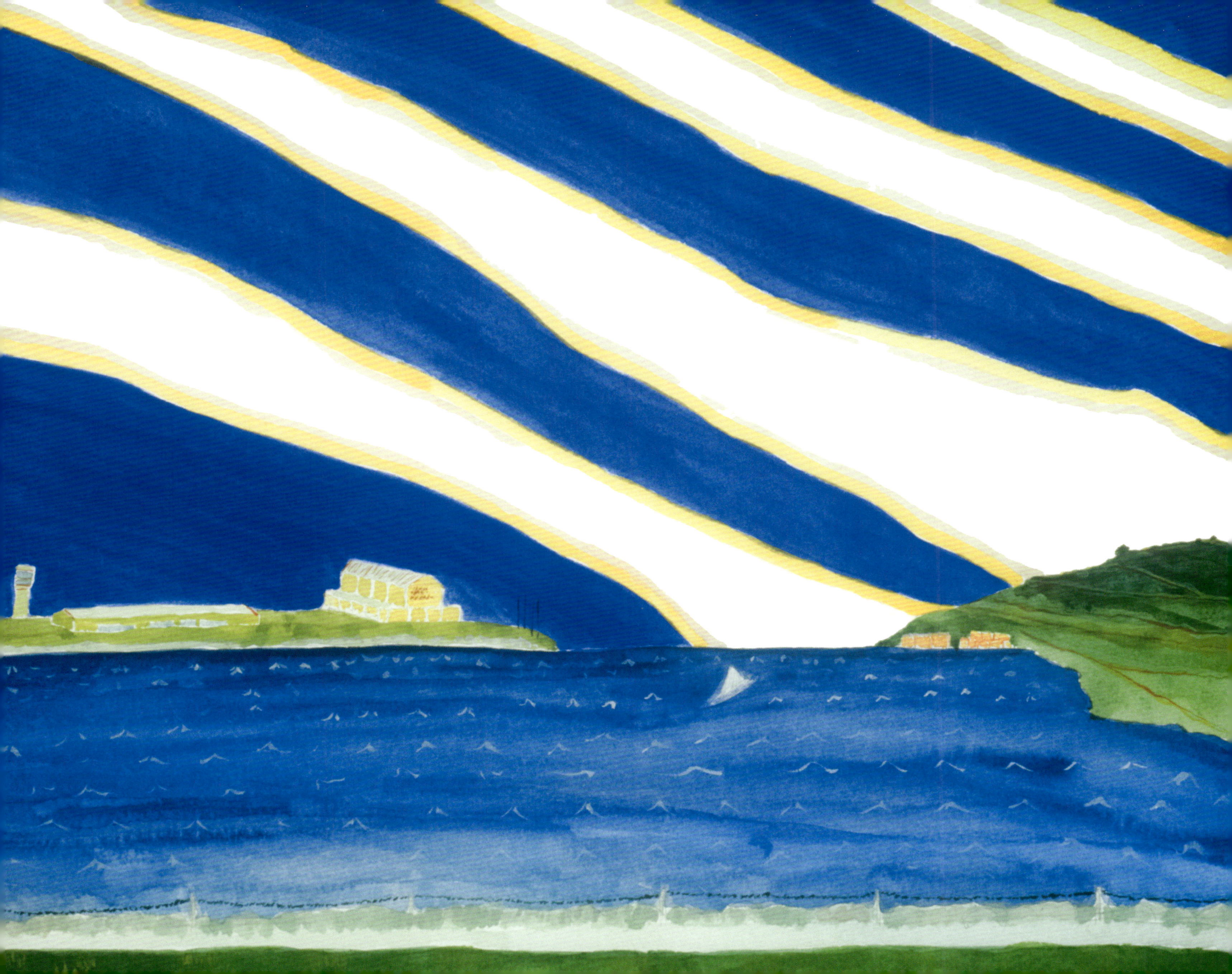

Erasing the Slate

Turning over
with a feather
a brown beetle,
stranded on his back
as he struggles
on the path,
you watch him
strut away,
whether to live
a long life
or a few straggling hours,
you do not
know
or foretell,
but rather care
that for an instant,
you and a bird's
cast-off
plumage
took the place
of a friendly
breeze,
taking time
to sweep clean
a road
for a stranger.

Tough Faith

An old woman
who smiles
from her nest
of wrinkles
gazes out
at the mountains –
what does she see
on their towering peaks,
except haloes
that have settled down
to sleep
in hard places?

Company

On a lonely
birthday,
a bird
darts out of the garden –
a flash
of blue and yellow
gives you the gift
of life
everlasting.

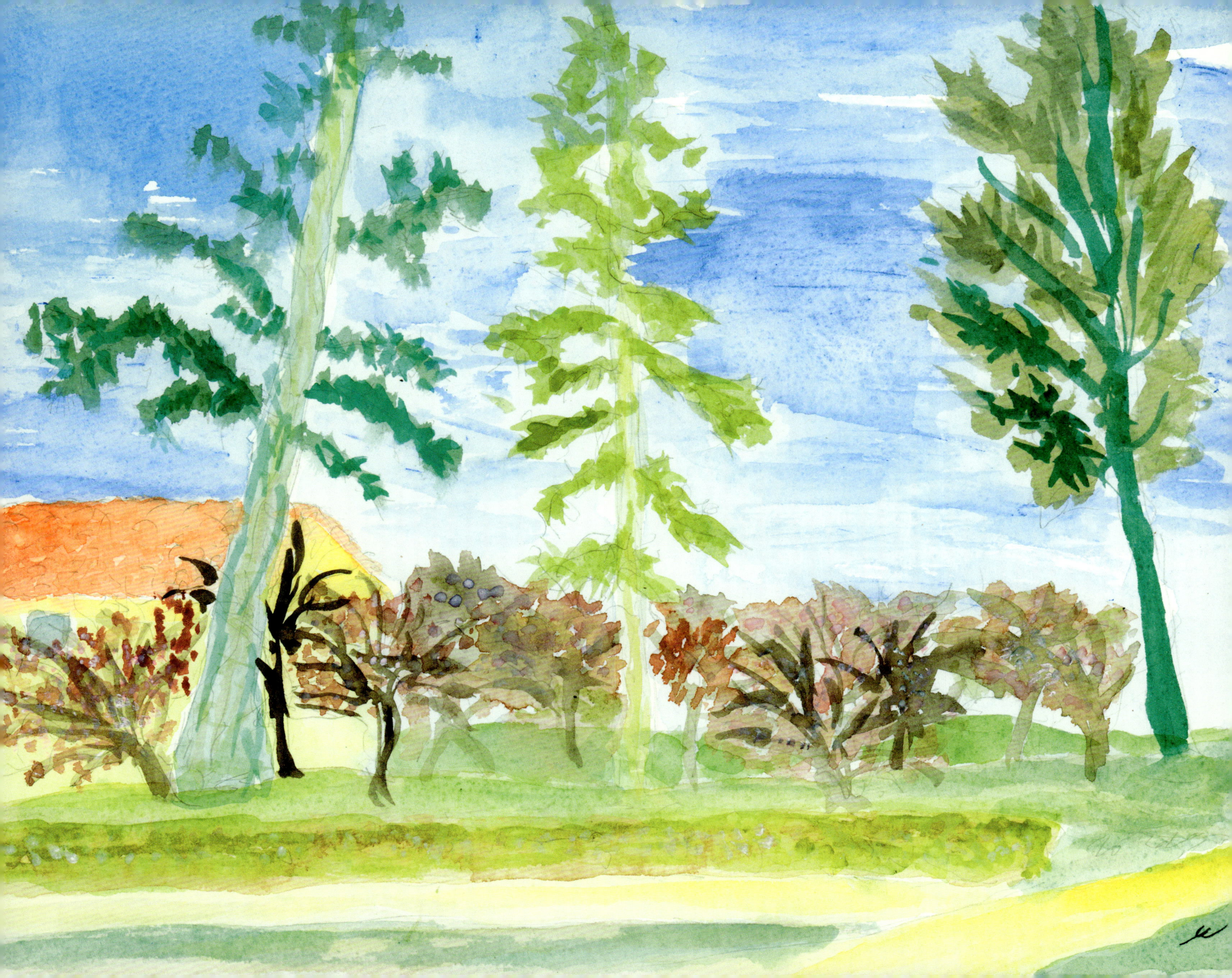

Winter Blessings

A rainstorm
over the ocean,
blossoming
in distant
sunlight,
offers its lavender-petaled
hydrangea clouds
to a garden
of purple
waves.

Tears
that drop
into a pool
of water
are not a waste
of salt
or speech,
for they signal
the farthest edge
of the universe
that they have replenished
a well
with a kiss
and a wink.

A Trio

An old man
whose wife
has passed away
talks
with a young woman
who has never
been married,
until an old matron,
hearing
their quiet
chat,
interrupts
them,
to ask
a question
of the woman
who has no secrets
yet
to share
with her children.

A Patient Custodian

Before the mountain,
fields
of yellow flowers
blossom,
stretching away
as far
as anyone can see –
above them
the sky
idles away
hours,
counting on clouds
to sweep clean
the land,
with downpours'
brooms
and shadows'
dry mops.

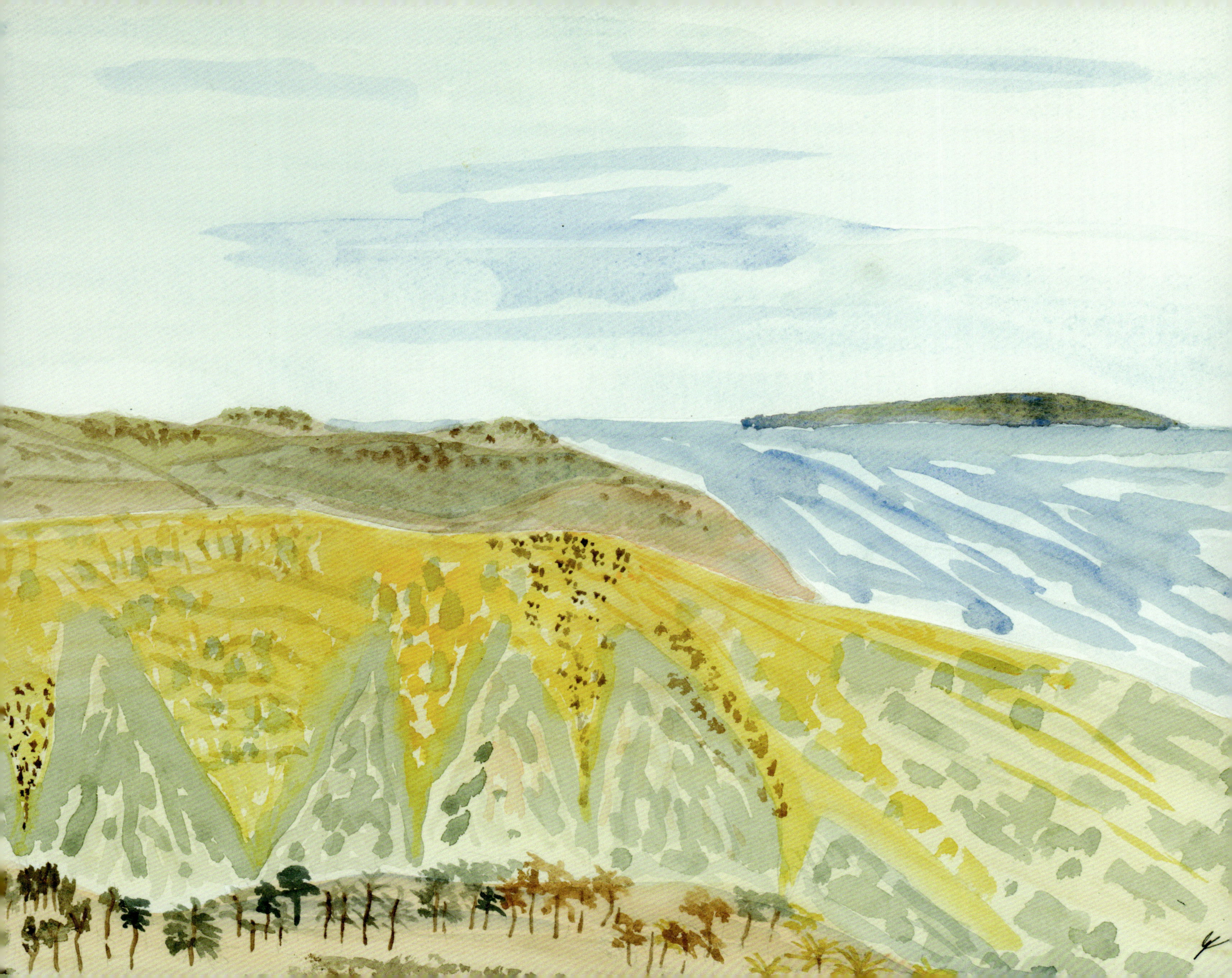

Enjoying the View

Sitting by the window,
in the summer sunlight
that glows
all afternoon,
you look out
at the bay
and the pastel hills,
and the pink spires
and the white ferry boats,
and the tumbledown
green hills,
and you are reconciled
in the westering light,
in the lap of a land
that has settled down
in sight
of a smiling
window.

Hannah Hollers

A father
with his toddler
laughs,
as she tosses high
a handful
of candy –
almost to Halloween,
the little girl
takes a deep breath,
then lets out
a scream
that makes nearby ghosts
dread
reincarnation.

Devotion

A widow
who lives
in a house
by the sea
points out the moonlight
that visits her
nightly,
as you gaze
out the window
at the far-flung
ocean,
which opens its arms
to a sky
where a cloud
and the moon
keep a tryst.

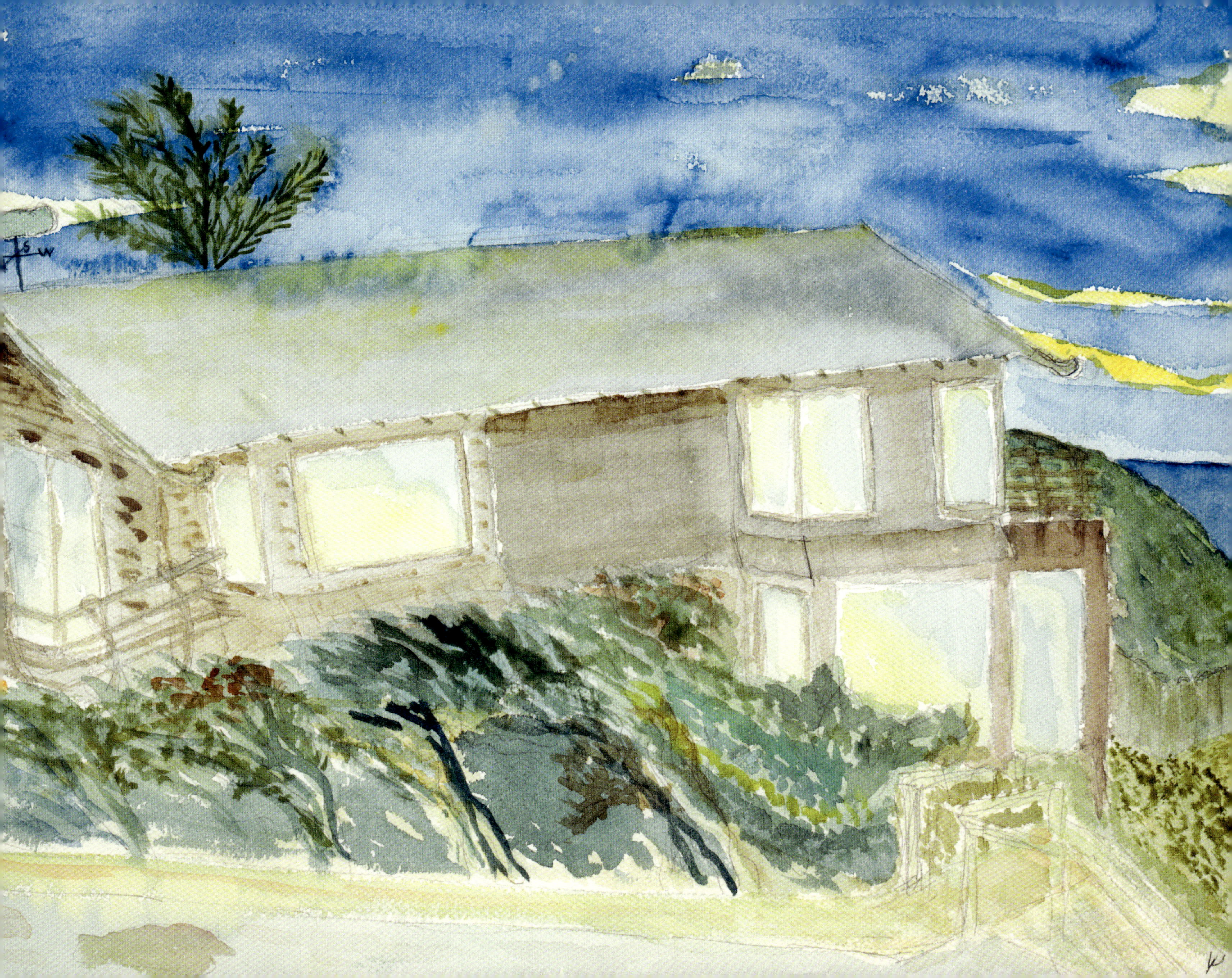

A Wake-Up Call

Running
at dawn,
you gulp down
the cool air,
and listen
to birds,
as they set notes
to their gossip.

Peaceful
half-light
drapes
about your shoulders –
your feet
rise and fall,
making music
with the pavement.

Peas in a Pod

A little boy,
asleep
beside his dad,
leans
his head
on his father's
arm
and dozes.

The future
can wait –
today
there is time
for two dreamers
to share
the same
peace of mind.

Welcome Arrivals

A long
afternoon,
lounging
on the beach,
stretches out
in lazy sunshine –
awaiting
calm breezes
and the lollygagging
light,
the hours
tell their stories
of an ocean
that has come calling
for a million
mornings.

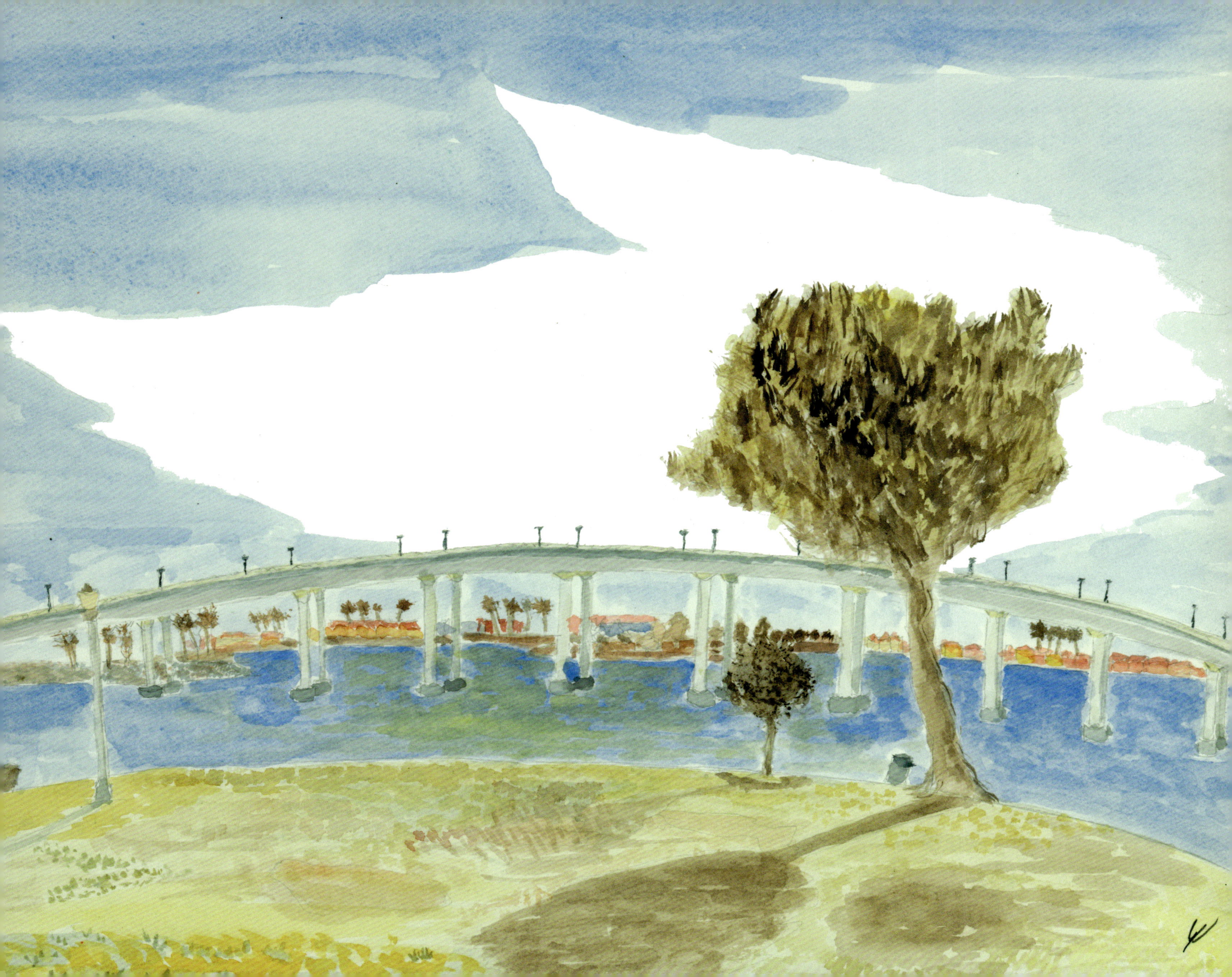

A First Date

On a quiet day
in March,
the trees
festoon themselves
with buds,
and, dancing
with breezes,
titter
among themselves,
sharing
their secrets
about shadows
that dress up
for spring.

A Joyful Noise

A quiet day
on the cusp
of spring
rests
among the shadows
of crisscrossing
boughs,
which wait
to dance
with the first
wayward breeze,
an aimless
traveler
with laughter
on its mind.

Bridging the Gap

An old bridge,
accustomed
to the clatter
of wagon wheels
and the clip-clop
of horse hooves,
makes room
for the grumbling
of autos
and the growling
of trucks,
and the whine
of rubber tires
that sputter their way
across the bridge,
which still connects
two sides
of a canyon,
friends
outstretching eucalyptus branches
to shade
passersby,
who stroll along
without a whisper
of complaint.

El Prado Bridge, Balboa Park

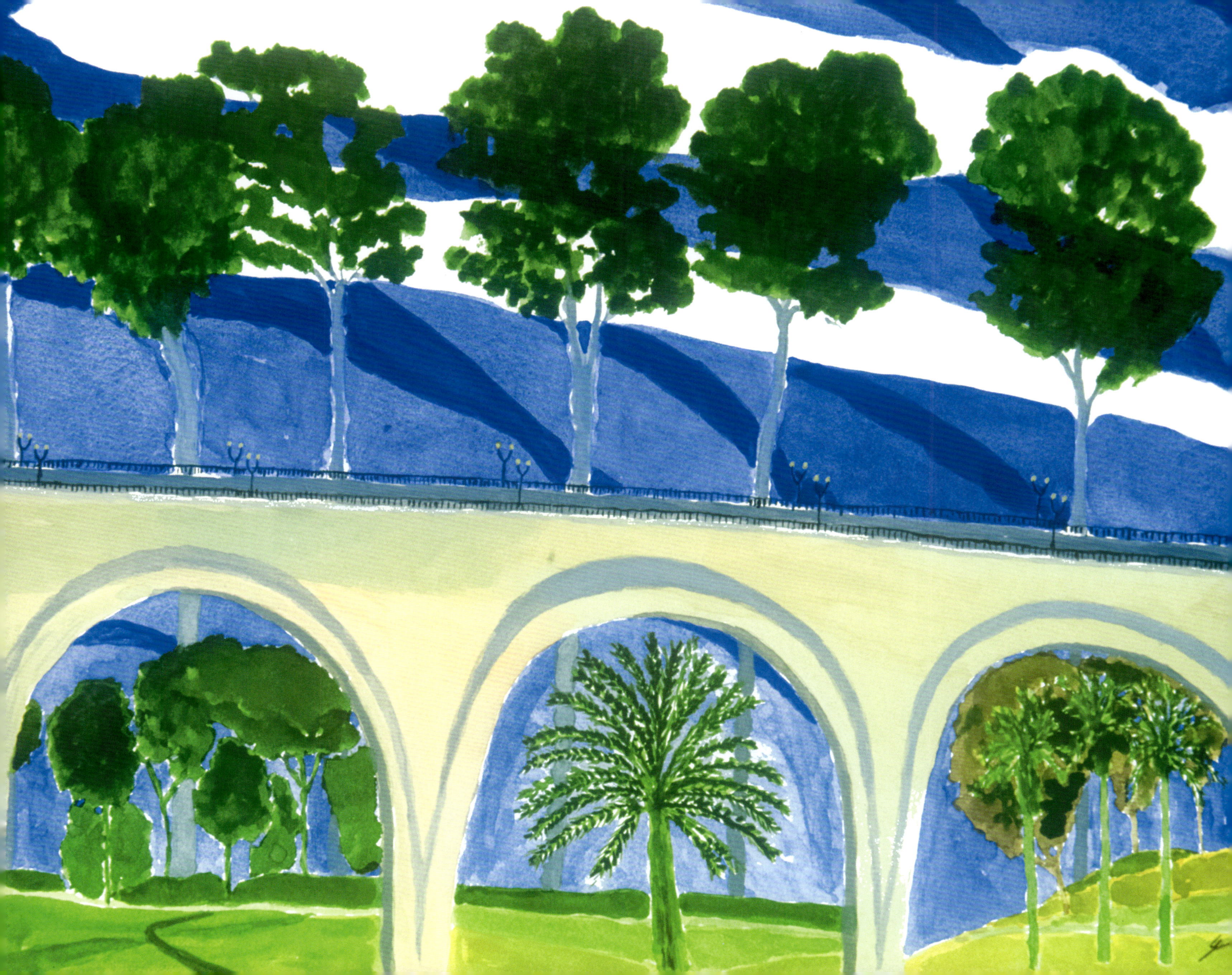

Night Navigation

At last
a star
appears,
and you give
thanks
for a clearing
at dusk –
a beacon,
lit
so long ago,
promises
laughter
at dawn.

Good Neighbors

Every March
the birds
build their nest
in a corner
of my rain gutter –
fluttering
and scratching
and twittering,
until the copper
softens
into straw –
unobtrusive
tenants,
they overpay
their rent –
they borrow
a few days' shelter,
while I,
seldom seeing them,
overhear
their fierce-hearted
housekeeping,
and take courage
between the rains.

Land Ho

An old lighthouse,
with its lantern
no longer ablaze,
welcomes a sky
that lights
its own torches,
and, beneath the firmament,
a blue-prowed ocean
that makes its way
safely
to shore.

A Bridal Beacon

An apple tree
blossoms
in the fog,
raising
pink arms
that brandish
lavender bouquets –
under the streetlamps
it makes the sky
glow,
lighting up
with a glance
its homegrown
cloud.

Happy Either Way

Three street people,
asleep
on a sunny day
in March,
sprawled out
in the arms
of warm grass,
know
better than any philosopher
why spring
is a miracle
or a dream.

Sharing a Secret

At last
the black-leafed
plum tree
has festooned itself
with lavender blossoms –
it was worth
the wait,
during winter storms
and spring squalls,
for now
the sky's
shy suitor
has raised
its soft fingertips,
to point out
an orchid
cloud.

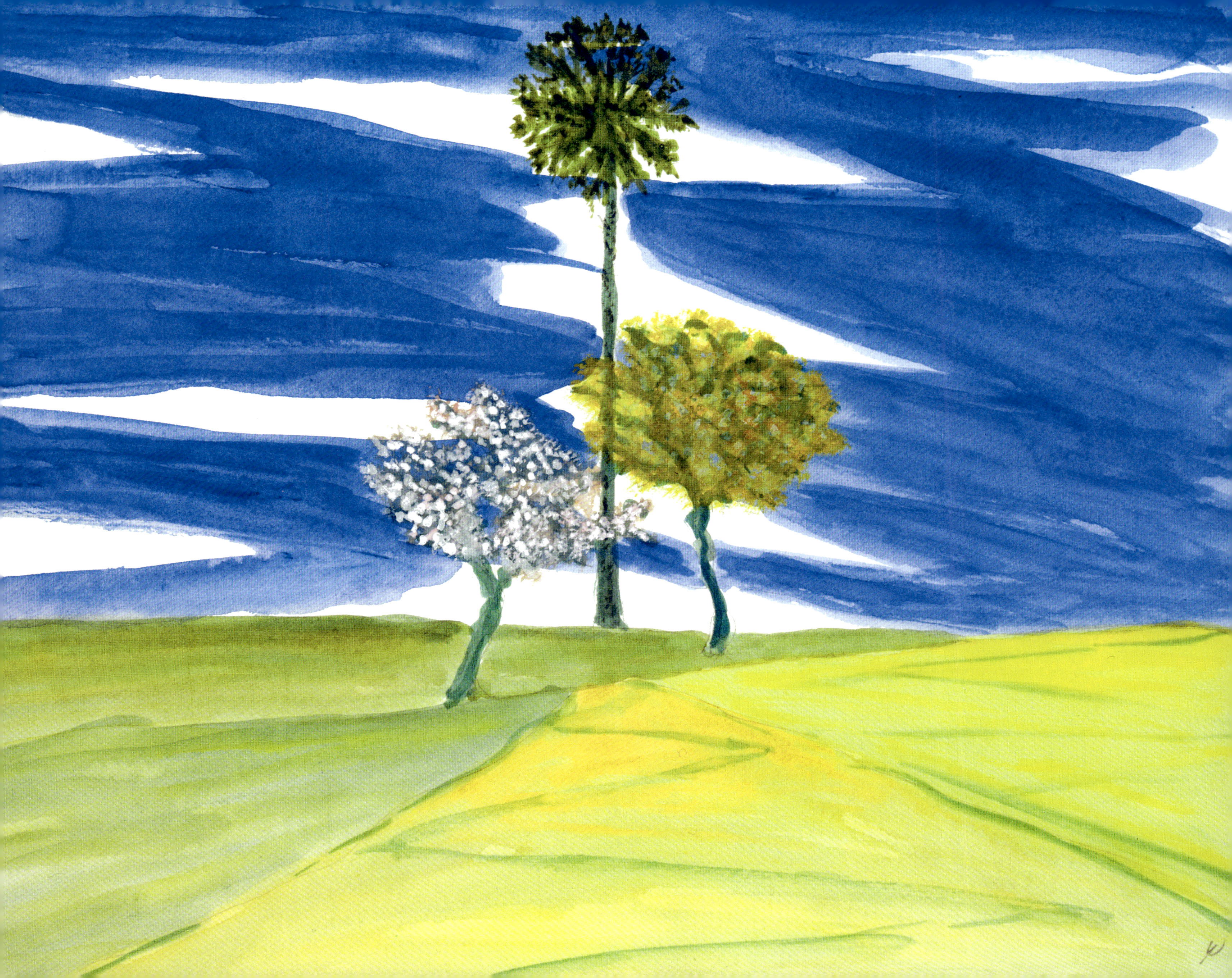

A Spring Field

The purple ocean
blossoms
at the horizon,
a sudden flower
beaming
beyond the green land –
unfolding
its bright petals,
it winks
at a wandering sky,
which gardens
in its spare time,
but never expects
the ocean
to dare the horizon
to smile.

Redemption

Pear trees
in blossom
in January,
brandishing
their torches
of hope,
embolden
the sky
to adorn itself
with strands
of clouds,
while the trees
have answered
a sputtering rain
with a downpour
of lavender petals
and perfume.

A Late Romance

Streamers
of orange
and red
and purple
festoon
the high-waved coast,
which welcomes the fall
of darkness,
so that the ocean may whisper
sweet nothings
to the stars.

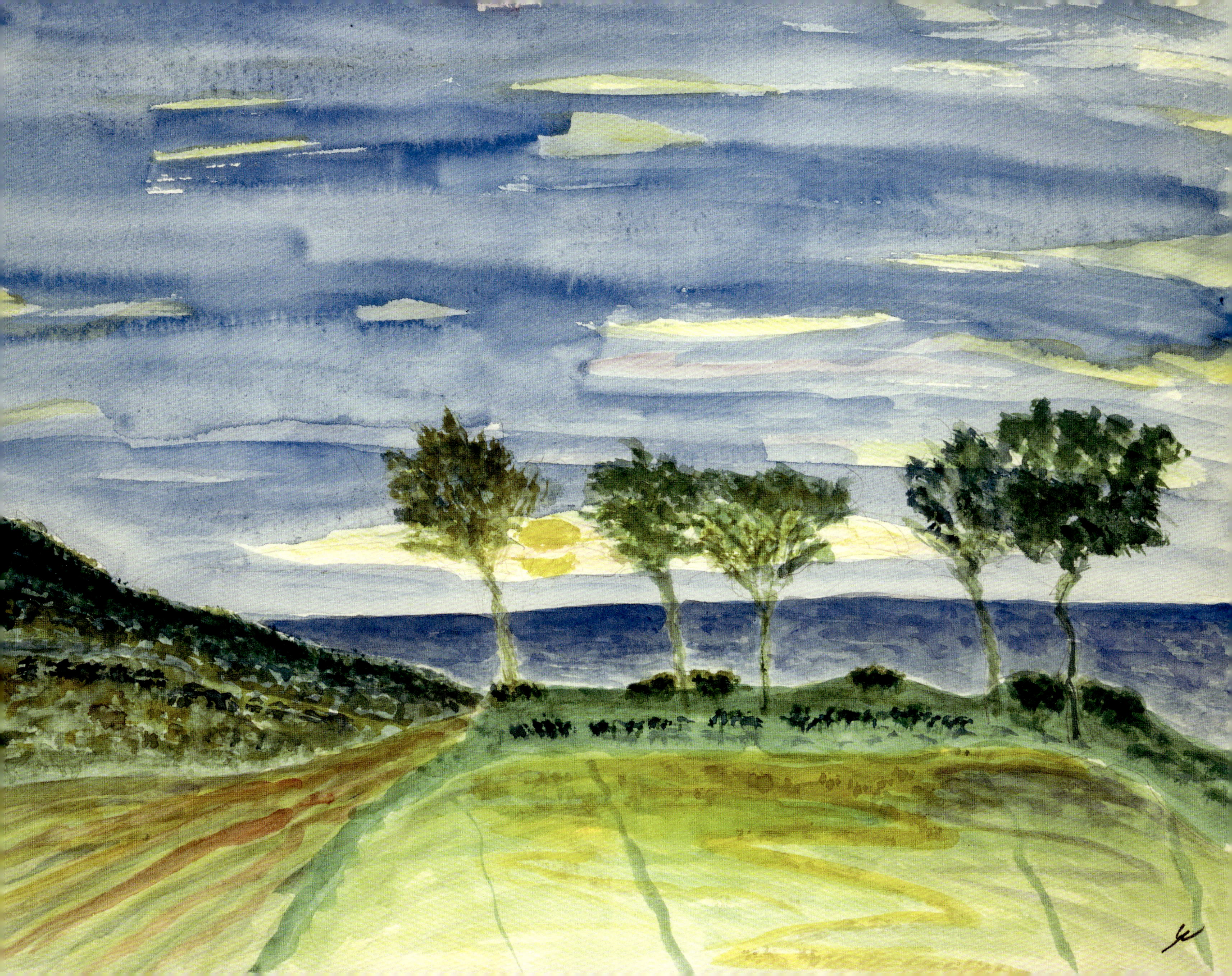

Setting Sail

Beyond the golden
beach,
the double-chinned breakers,
and the sunlit sailboats,
the horizon,
all waves
and light,
promises
a union
between the distance
and your last
footfall
on the wide-eyed
shore.

June Slumber

Clouds
over the ocean
mask
the great waves,
the bobbing ships,
the seagulls
and the flying
fish –
the ocean
wears
its summer
coverlet,
a white eiderdown
so soft
that the waves
do not bother
to kick it off
at dusk.

All night
the moonlight
embroiders it
with silver lace,
and in the morning,
it has been rolled up,
and the ocean
dozes
under naked
sunlight.

At Rest

Two catamarans,
drawn up
on an orchid
beach,
wait
for a high tide
to lure them
away,
to an island
that harbors
endless light,
hiding behind
the shyest
of palm fans.

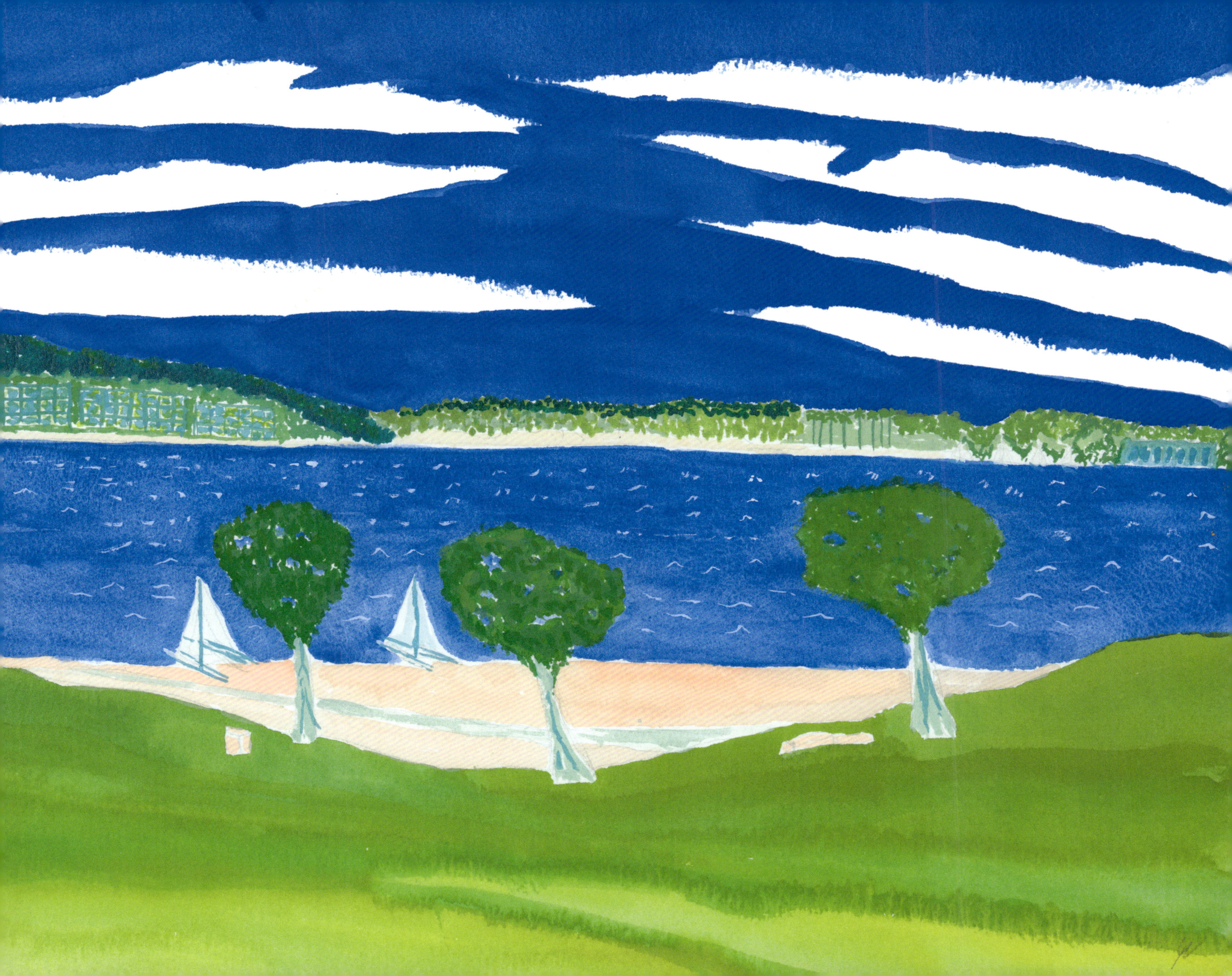

Heading West

At last
the sky clears,
and the land
stretches out
forever –
beyond the storm clouds,
roads
cross the horizon,
while fields
turn down
their covers,
as fences
rise and fall
on hillsides,
and the air,
as sweet
as spring blossoms,
creeps
through open windows,
which welcome
dawdling breezes,
left behind
by gray-bearded storms
that have important business
east of here.

Conversion

Plowed fields
at the edge
of the desert
promise
a fresh beginning,
a hope
that lightning
will strike
barbed wire,
and thunderheads
in August
will start
bawling.

Warner Ranch

A valley
at the edge
of the mountains
hangs out to dry
its tawny coat,
its corduroy
vest,
and its faded
blue jeans –
soon enough
someone comes calling,
a kicking-up-her-heels
breeze,
bringing
laughter
and hot-breathed
dancing.

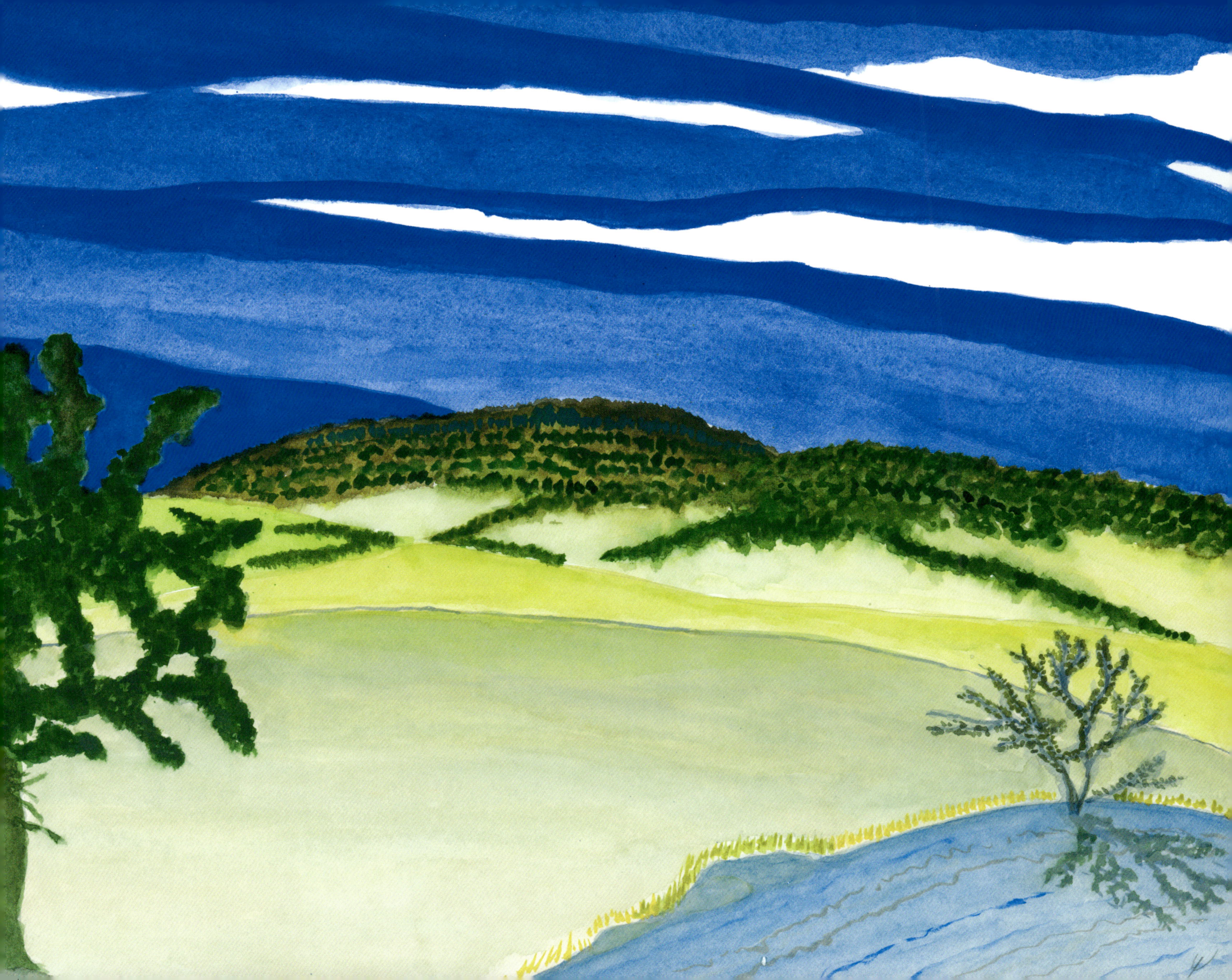

Fortune Hunters

Overturned
leaves,
with dewdrops
in their palms,
snatch
the sunlight,
then give back
to the sky
a fistful
of diamonds.

Crusaders

An eight-year-old boy
runs across the field,
crying out
to a playmate,
"Look! A gulley!"

Dashing
back and forth
across it,
they whoop
at one another,
chasing clumps of turf
up and down,
storming
a castle
on a day
when the crocodiles
have drunk dry
the moat.

A Spendthrift Lover

Sweet-scented
eucalyptus boughs,
spreading
their lemon
perfume,
open their arms
to the summer night,
which has thrown away
a fortune
in stars.

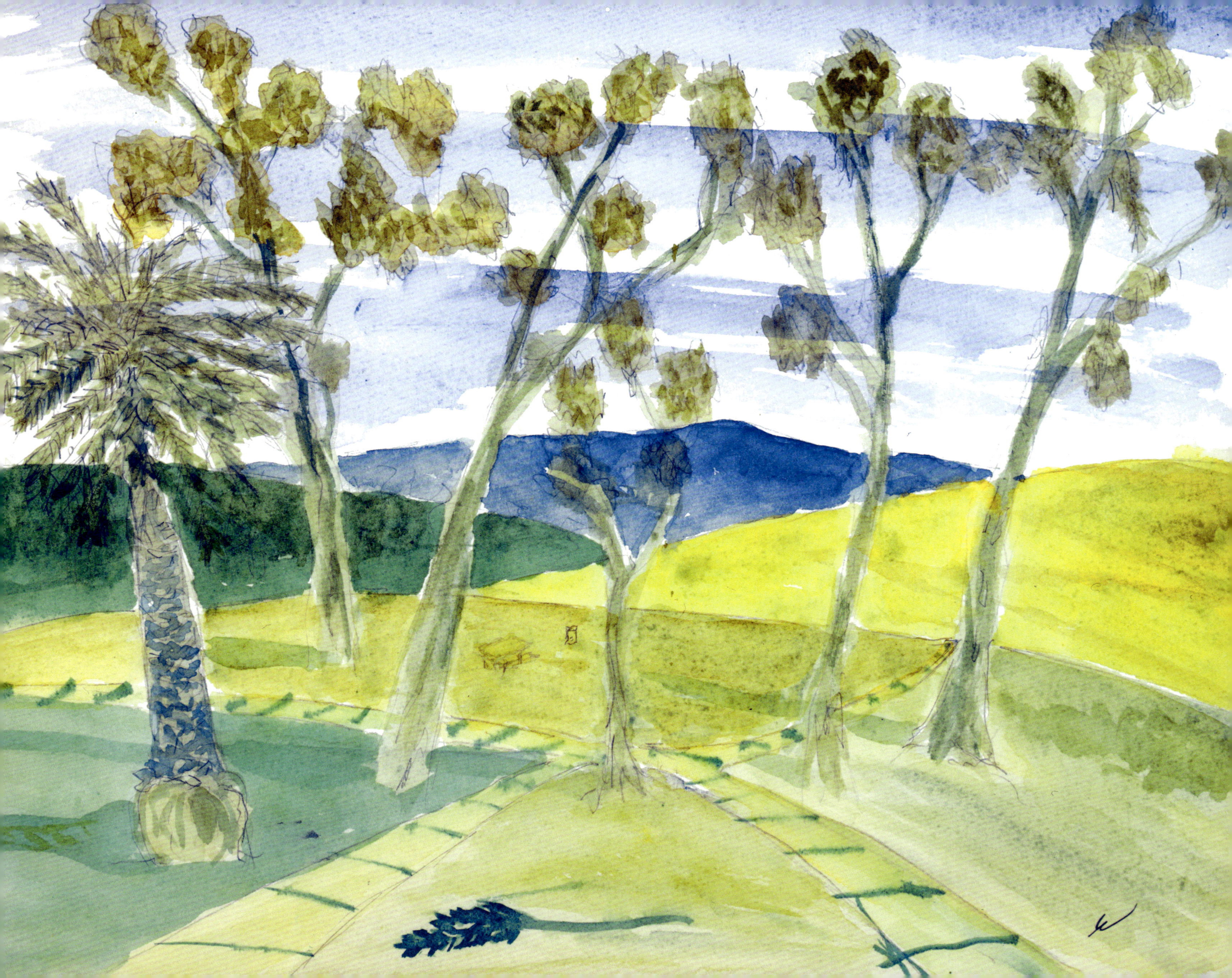

True Enough

Lavender blossoms
on a black-barked
fruit tree
outstretch
their handfuls
of confetti
to breezes
that, still cool-hearted,
stir
the dots of petals
that confront
an ice-blue sky,
until the wind
scatters them
upon a gray sidewalk
that has waited
for months
to blush.

A Holy Truce

Religions discuss
one god and another,
all of them formidable,
all of them comforting,
and decide at last
to rely
upon prayer,
where no one can know
who is listening
or answering.

A Cordial Tummy

A paunchy
friendship bell,
seldom rung,
reserves
its bass voice
for curious strangers,
who climb over a fence
and thump it
on the stomach,
then smile
to hear it
grumble
its approval.

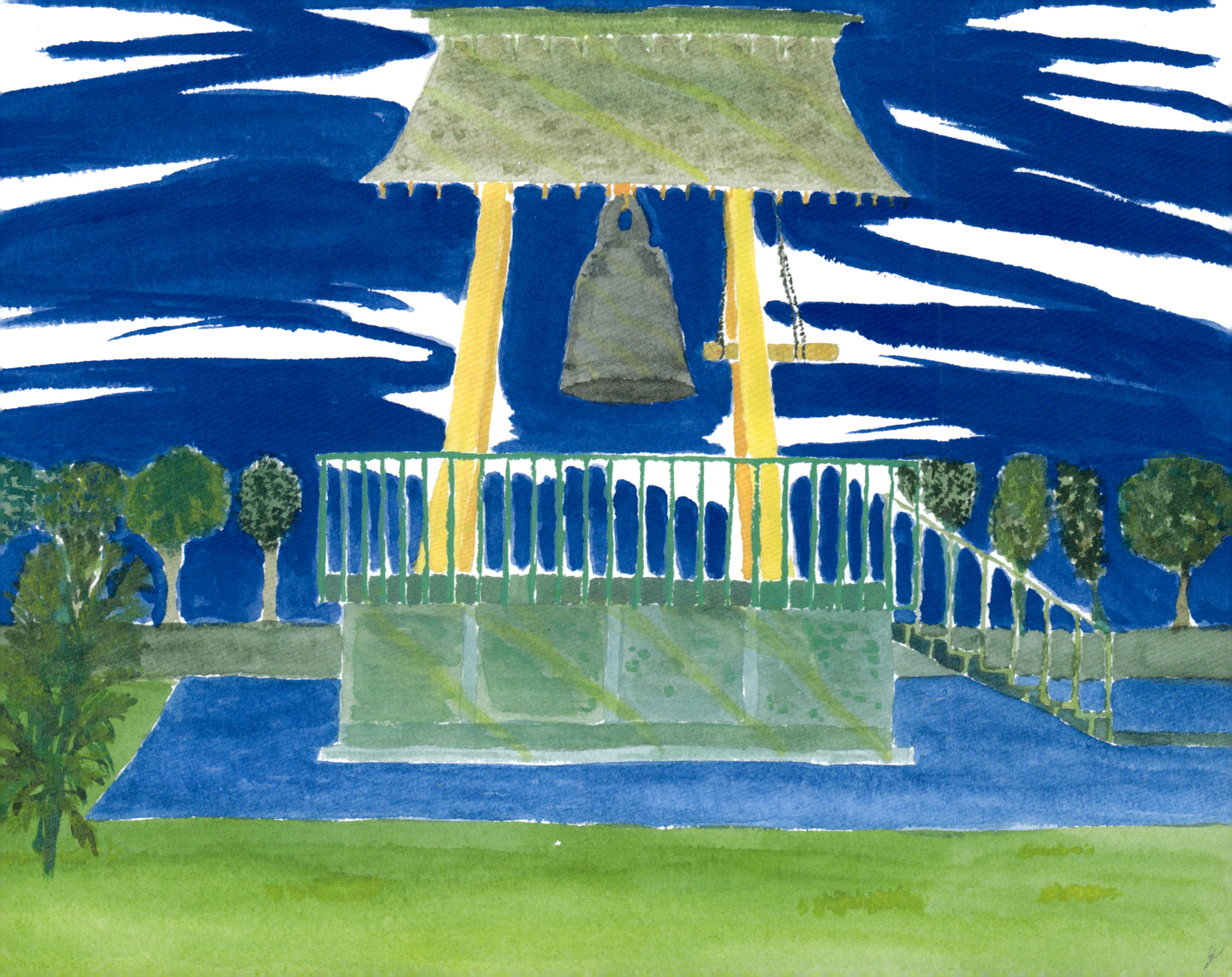

Settling Down

The sunlit afternoon
fades
beside the quiet bay,
where freighters
and ferries
paint the waves
with their white wakes,
and the slopes
of the hills
sparkle,
wearing necklaces
of houses,
and the day
slips into evening,
as the streets
hang up their Japanese
lanterns,
and the bay
covers its mirror
with a purple veil,
and stars
chart a course
for light-starved
harbors.

Hot Stuff

A freighter
out at sea,
gray-hulled
and graceful,
knives
through the waves,
as the light
glides before it,
and when a sleek rainbow
follows its stern,
the ship
heads for the horizon,
as if for an island
in need of news
and refrigerators.

Never Too Late

Light
on the horizon
after the storm
pries its way
into a gap
between clouds
and the ocean –
a single-eyed
beacon
of dazzling
hope,
it makes room
for a western glow
that beds down
with purple waves,
while a ship
holds its course
to a land
abandoned
to sunlight.

View from Pt. Loma

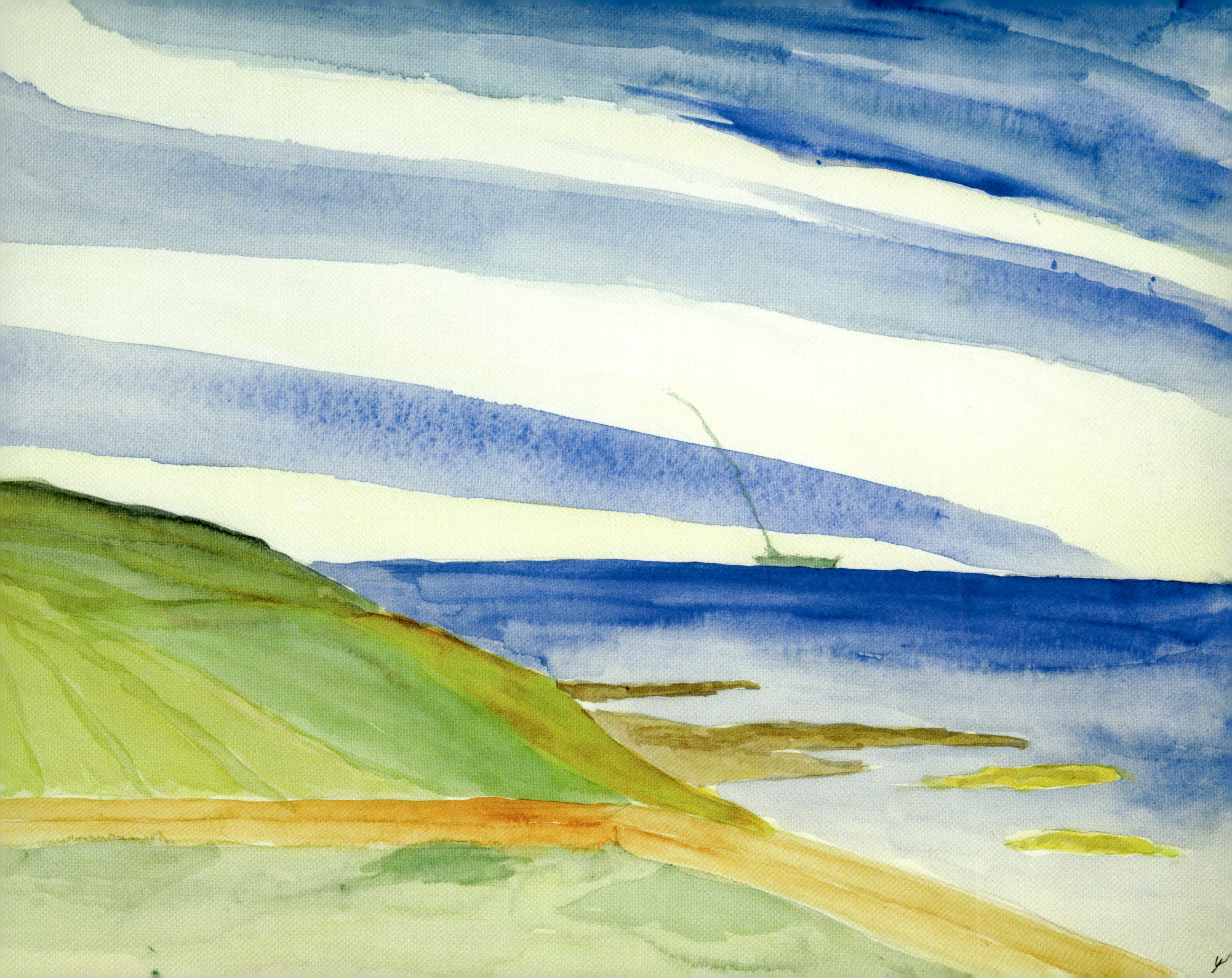

Our Wildest Dreams

Along the golden coast,
seagulls
glide
in formation
at sunset,
while wayfarers
watch
from the steepest
bluffs
the sun's
taillights streak
down a thoroughfare
west.

Interior Design

Two lovers
sit
in the park
at dusk,
arguing
about the color
of the kitchen –
one holds
the advantage,
the silent
threat
to move on,
until the other
puts his arm
around his partner's
shoulder,
and in a moment,
they stroll away,
through the silence
of a perfectly-painted
orange and purple
sky.

Dancing with Dusk

The last
of the light,
fading
out of the sky,
leaves
the clouds
to their garden
of orchids,
to their soft-petaled
forest,
while the horizon
unfurls
its butterfly wings,
to carry away
the weight
of the world.

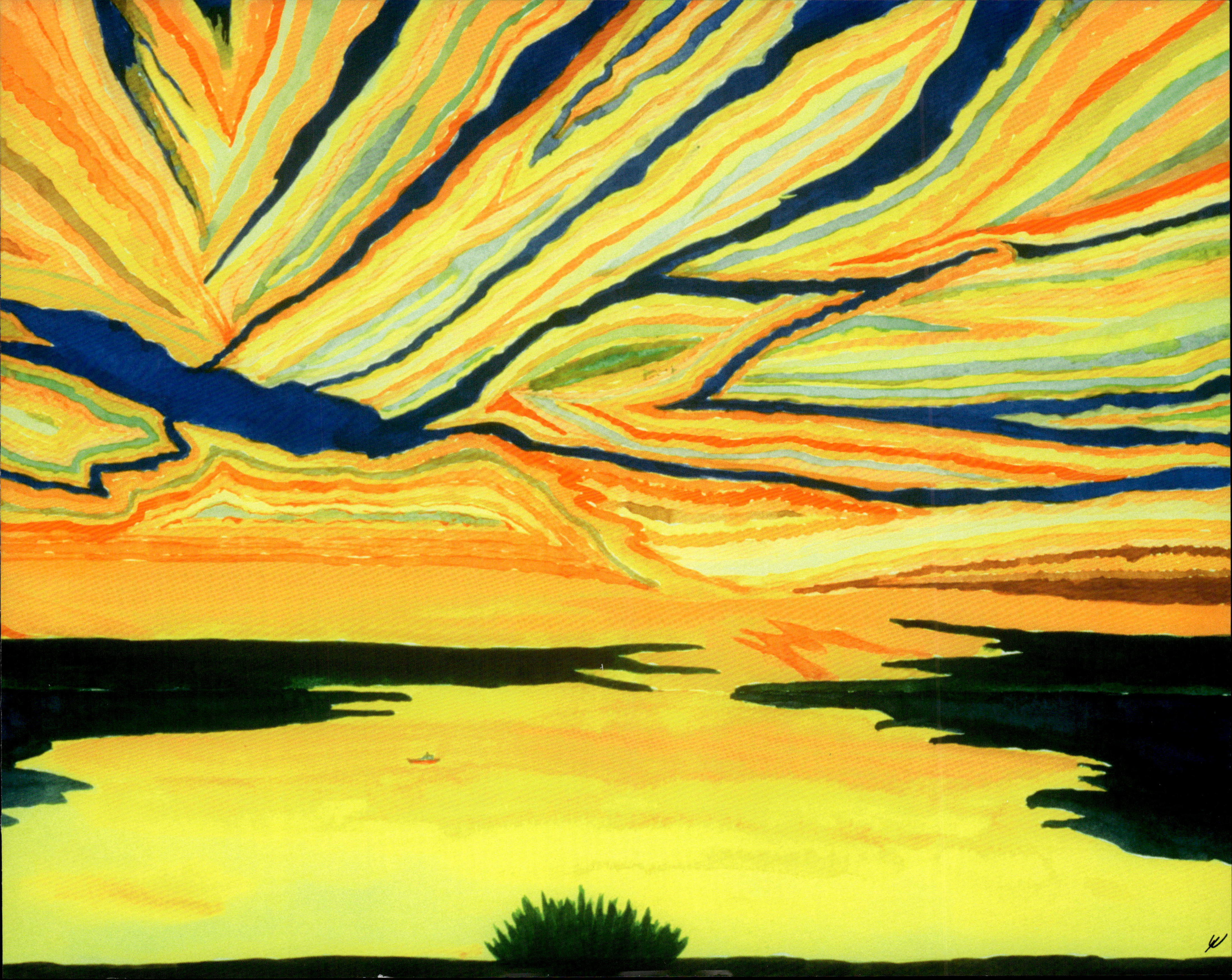